CONTENTS

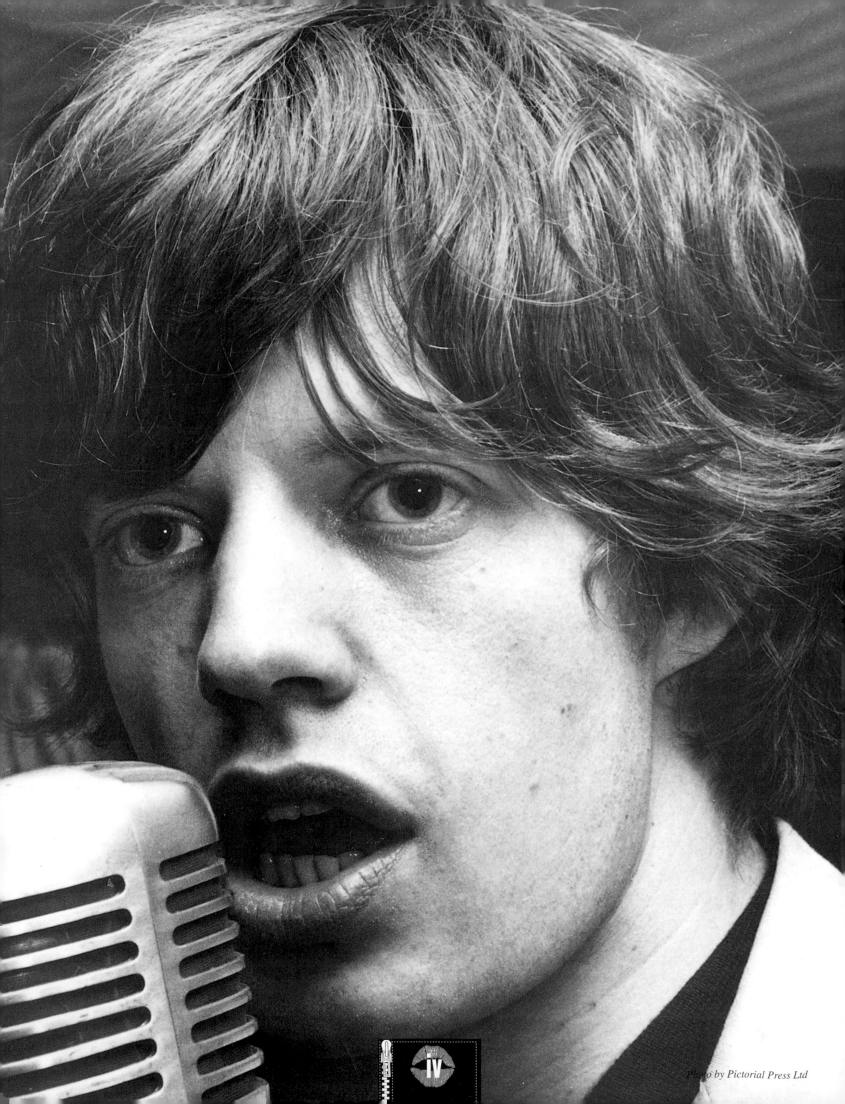

$\mathcal{A}$cknowledgements

I remember how the teen mags and radio stations back in the 1960s always had the Beatles versus the Stones. It was Elvis versus Cliff before that, but this was the era of the beat groups. Like many teenagers at the time, I was lucky enough to witness the rise of the greatest rock 'n' roll band in the world, from seeing them live on stage in Tunbridge Wells to queuing at the local record store for their latest '45'. They were indeed exciting times, and in writing this book I have tried to recapture that excitement.

For this, an unauthorised biography of their first ten years, I have drawn on documentary materials and interviews with the Stones themselves, as well as recollections from those who knew them or worked with them during that period. I have also included some of my own personal recollections as well as material from books and other memorabilia. But for making it all possible, I really must thank a number of people: they are Phil Scott, who saw the project through from beginning to end, Peter Lewry, who suggested Castle Communications in the first place, Andrew King for his advice and guidance, Keith Hayward and his sister Janet for their research brilliance and fortitude, and Kate King for her invaluable word processing and enthusiasm.

I would also like to thank a number of friends who have put up with me 'going on' about the Stones while I was writing this book: Nick King, Alan Lucas and his lovely wife Clair, and one of my longest and dearest friends Vivienne Singer. Also Gill Watson and last but not least, my mother, who was totally shocked by the Stones' first television appearance on *Thank Your Lucky Stars*. I think she's still recovering from their long hair!

Finally, I would like to dedicate this book to all those friends and colleagues, and of course to the Rolling Stones.

Nigel Goodall

Keith Richards, 1966 • Photo by Pictorial Press Ltd

INTRODUCTION

The Early Days

I t was a cold October day in 1960 when Mick Jagger, travelling to the London School of Economics, and Keith Richards, on his way to Sidcup Art College, ran into each other on Dartford Railway Station. It would be the first time since their days at Wentworth County Primary School that they had seen each other, and today they would rekindle their friendship through their discovery of a mutual love and affection for American rhythm and blues.

Michael Philip Jagger was born on 26 July 1943, in Dartford, Kent. His father, Basil Joe Jagger, came from Lancashire, and his mother, Eva Mary, was born in Australia. Mick went to Wentworth Junior County Primary School, where he made his early friendship with Keith Richards, who had been born on 18 December 1943, to staunch working-class parents.

'We lived on the same block for a while when we were kids,' recalls Mick. 'Another guy who lived on the block was the painter Peter Blake, but it was a pretty rough block. Keith and I went to the same school at one point and we walked home together. Then I met him later on and we really remembered each other.'

After completing school, Mick won a scholarship to the London School of Economics to study law, and it was during his time there that he met up with Keith again. Their regular get-togethers eventually resulted in a band, Boy Blue and the Blue Boys. The pair formed the band together with school chums Dick Taylor, Bob Beckwith and Allan Etherington and concentrated on imitating the early recordings of Jimmy Reed and Chuck Berry. 'I can remember Mick practising with a group of boys outside our house in Beckwith,' recalls Mrs Taylor, Jagger's neighbour and mother of group member, Dick Taylor. 'We used to sit in the next room and crease up with laughter. It was lovely, but so loud. I always heard more of Mick than I saw of him. I didn't dream they were serious. I thought it was just for fun.' At this time Mick was still supposedly studying at the LSE and he dragged himself there just often enough to avoid being thrown out and losing his college grant.

Keith was far more into imagery than Mick at this time. He had already been through his 'teddy boy' period, wearing drainpipe trousers and lurid pink socks, while he was at Dartford Technical College before going on to do three years at Sidcup College of Art.

At the time Keith met Mick, teenagers were slowly being turned on to the blues, signalling a major musical shift away from jazz. The giants of this new music were people like Howling Wolf and Muddy Waters.

In Britain Chris Barber, jazz band leader, co-founder of the first working skiffle group and blues lover of many years' standing, decided he wanted to include a taster of this new American music in his show. Eventually settling for a Chicago Blues spot for his wife, Odele Paterson, he got in touch with Alexis Korner, who, by early 1959, had earned himself a name for playing the blues; real blues. Alexis was introduced to Cyril Davies.

'In our search for a guitarist who understood the blues, Chris couldn't think of a practising expert guitar player, but he did know a fan who could play the guitar,' recalls Harold Pendleton, Chris's business associate and at that time the manager of the Marquee Club in London. 'He'd known Alexis for many years. He'd been to all our concerts when we brought in people like Sonny and Brownie, Muddy Waters and so on. Chris realised that Alexis knew what was required, so we dropped the horns, trumpet, clarinet and trombone and added Cyril and Alexis to the rhythm section. We started these half-hour sets of rhythm and blues down at the Marquee on a Wednesday night, which the audience really seemed to appreciate.'

As time progressed, Alexis earned himself a name for playing with people like Ken Coyler, and also for running the London Club known as the Blues and the Barrelhouse; but eventually he wanted to break away musically with his own group. He had never really been that comfortable with the jazz part of Barber's set, so the split was not altogether surprising. However, Korner quickly found that there was a lack of clubs and venues prepared to book anything other than jazz bands. He was also aware that there was a huge audience of rhythm and blues fans waiting to be captured, so he decided to start his own club in Ealing Broadway, calling it the Ealing Club. Soon his band, Blues Incorporated, was playing to capacity audiences in the back room, behind the ABC Bakery.

Meanwhile, Mick and Keith were rehearsing with their band in Kent, and a brilliant guitarist from Cheltenham called Brian Jones was looking for the chance to play the interval spot for Blues Incorporated. He got in touch with Korner and pleaded to be given the opportunity.

Brian Lewis Hopkins-Jones was born on 28 February 1942, to Lewis Blont and Louise Beatrice Jones. Lewis worked as an aeronautical engineer and Louise taught the piano. Brian attended Dean Close Public School as a day boy before going to Cheltenham Grammar, where he was suspended for a short time after encouraging rebellion against prefects, though he managed to leave with nine 'O' levels and two 'A' levels. By 1958 Brian's interest in music had led him to be the secretary of the local 66 Jazz Club. By then, he was playing saxophone in several local jazz bands including Bill Nile's Delta Jazz Band. This was followed by a spell with the Ramrods, a rock band that played gigs at local dances and art schools. Brian became estranged from his family after leaving several young girls

Alexis Korner • Photo by Pictorial Press Ltd

On HMS Discovery, London Embankment, 1963 • Photo by Tony Gale/Pictorial Press Ltd

pregnant and, rather than go to university, he chose to work, starting out with a job on the buses, then as a coalman and finally in a record shop.

Alexis could not deny Brian his break, so in March 1962 Brian sat in with Korner's band for the first time. By chance, Korner had also invited Mick, who like Brian, had asked to fill the interval slot.

'I remember when Mick and Keith first came down to the club,' recalls Long John Baldry, who was at that time the vocalist of Blues Incorporated. Basically Mick's repertoire was all Chuck Berry things, but the first thing I ever heard him play and sing was "Beautiful Delilah". Keith had a tatty old guitar then, but then I don't think anybody had particularly good electric guitars at that time. Even so, Keith's was pretty primitive. It was at that same time that I can remember Brian coming down from Cheltenham, but he wasn't playing electric guitar then, as far as I recall he played acoustic.'

1963 • Photo by Rex Features Ltd

It was not until Brian grabbed a second spot guesting with Blues Incorporated on 7 April that he met Mick, Keith and Dick Taylor. That meeting allowed the guys that would eventually form the greatest rock 'n' roll band in the world to acquaint themselves with each other. But Brian had already made plans to start his own band. He had placed an advertisement in *Jazz News* asking for interested musicians to attend a rehearsal. Jagger and company were not invited to drop by so, for the time being at least, Mick, Keith and Dick continued their visits to the Ealing Club, with Mick sitting in with Alexis's band whenever he could.

'It was ever so wet,' remembers Mick, 'so wet that Cyril had to put a sort of horrible sheet up over the bandstand so the condensation didn't drip directly on us – it just dripped through the sheet onto us instead of directly. It was very dangerous too, because of all the electricity and microphones but I never got a shock'.

'It was so primitive . . . and there was old Alexis with his guitar with a pick-up across it. I remember scenes with John Baldry and Paul Jones, who was very cool in those days. He used to get up there with shades on, trying to be ever so cool with a donkey jacket, but he used to sing quite nicely quite sort of mature. I could never get in key – it was always a problem 'cos I was quite often drunk. The first time I sang down there I was really nervous because I'd never sung in public before. I remember I used to sing "Got My Mojo Working" with John Baldry and Paul Jones sometimes, but they were all much taller than me so I always used to feel very small. But that was at the very beginning of everything. Tuesday nights down there were amazing, about six people used to come and it was so cold that we had to play with our coats on.'

In the meantime Brian was auditioning the musicians who had responded to his *Jazz News* advertisement. One musician who dropped by to take a look was a boogie-woogie pianist from Cheam in Surrey, called Ian Stewart. 'From my point of view the Stones started with Brian really, in that he was the first one I met. There was only him and a couple of other guys at the rehearsal. He didn't like the piano player he'd got, so I just started playing piano and we went through different people. This was at a time when the Ealing thing was starting, and of course Brian knew Alexis, so he got to know Mick, Keith and Charlie.'

In no time at all Ian became Brian's anchorman and friend. He quickly discovered that though Mick and Keith were almost inseparable as friends, Mick's singing with Alexis's band had come between them somewhat. Ian figured that the offer to join Brian's band would be enough to get both down to rehearsals. 'So we had this group with Mick and Keith and they brought Dick Taylor and we used to get any drummer we could find. We didn't really get Charlie with us for a long time because he was playing with another group that was making money and Charlie needed the money. We must have used eight or nine different drummers, but we didn't really play in public at all. In fact, we sometimes went weeks without playing because we just didn't seem to be getting anywhere. I remember Brian would get pissed off with it and vanish, so eventually we thought about starting clubs ourselves, in pubs, the way jazz clubs were at the time.'

By June 1962 Alexis's Blues Incorporated were a big enough live name to attract the attention of the BBC and their *Jazz Club* radio show. Korner was approached to do the show, but that in itself created a problem – the broadcast clashed with the group's Thursday night residency at the Marquee. There was, however, a compromise. It was agreed that Mick would get Brian's band together for the gig and still be the familiar frontman. It was thought that no-one would notice if the backing line-up had changed. Brian was not happy that it was Jagger's status that had swung the gig for them, but he accepted the booking all the same. To make sure his authority as the band's leader was not being overlooked, Brian insisted on choosing the name of the group.

'The Rolling Stones' was taken from a favourite Muddy Waters song, 'Rollin' Stone Blues'. They all hated it, but accepted it because it was, after all, Brian who had formed the group. Now the band were to make their first London appearance with the line-up of Mick on vocals, Keith and Brian on guitars, Dick Taylor on bass, Ian on piano and Mick Avory on drums.

They were aware that this was their live debut at the Marquee, and that it was going to be tough from the minute they walked out onto the dimly lit stage. The atmosphere was decidedly uneasy. The audience were not about to be taken in by an unknown band of scruffy R&B imitators; however, they very quickly warmed to the Stones' performance until, about half-way through, a large group of Mods appeared. They eyed everyone up and down, then pushed their way forward to the front of the stage causing unrest with the regulars. The Mods admired the way that Keith and Brian were playing the Chuck Berry riffs, then they gleefully attacked the audience. Violent chaos followed.

None of this, however, deterred the Ealing Club from booking the Rolling Stones for a spot which proved to be their most important breakthrough, leading to a succession of five other gigs in as many weeks. These gigs enhanced the band's reputation and popularity to such a level that even the Marquee took a risk in putting them on for a second time.

By now Mick, Brian and Keith had found a flat to share at 102 Edith Grove in Fulham. It was completely run down, damp and cold. Bare lightbulbs hung down from the yellow decaying ceilings and the wallpaper peeled off the walls in sheets. The communal toilet was accessible only by candle light, and the most frequent visitors there were rats. They would scatter along the skirting boards whenever anyone entered. 'You just wouldn't want to live there,' remembers Keith. 'It was disgusting: mould growing on the walls and no-one was ever going to clean the joint up. We lived on the second floor and on the ground floor were these four students. Chick teachers from Sheffield and Nottingham who got roped into doing the cleaning, and occasionally got knocked off for their trouble.'

It would become worse as the harsh winter of 1962 set in. The plumbing would freeze solid, the lavatory would not flush and icicles would hang down like beaded curtains in every window and doorway.

Charlie Watts, 1964 • Photo by Pictorial Press Ltd

1963 • Photo by Pictorial Press Ltd

8

In the meantime, the Stones had started a club at the Red Lion public house in Sutton, where they kicked off with a Saturday night and Sunday afternoon gig. It was here, on 7 December that Bill Wyman, a bass player from Cheltenham, came along to see if he wanted to take the place of Dick Taylor, who by now had been dismissed from the band.

William George Perks was born on 24 October 1936 to William and Kathleen, a working-class couple from south-east London. At eighteen he was called up for National Service and entered the RAF, leaving two years later with a change of name to Bill Wyman, inspired by an RAF pal. By 1962, he was playing bass semi-professionally in a band called the Cliftons, who backed the then impressively billed 'England's answer to Little Richard', a lacklustre singer who went under the unfortunate name of Dickie Pride. Bill was older than the other Stones, with a wife, Diana, and a baby son, Stephen, something caused Brian to raise an eyebrow, but no more.

Brian auditioned Bill a few days later but was more impressed by the bass player's equipment than by his actual playing ability. Bill had a huge Vox 850 bass cabinet as well as his show-stealing Vox Phantom bass. His first gig with the Rolling Stones was on 15 December at a youth club in Putney. Then, after a gig at the Ricky Tic club in Windsor, and without thinking too much about the consequences, Brian got rid of their drummer in an attempt to get Charlie Watts to join the band. He too had been playing with Alexis's Blues Incorporated.

'I met Alexis in a club somewhere,' remembers Charlie. 'And he asked me if I'd play drums for him. A friend of mine, Andy Webb, said I should join the band, but I had to go to Denmark to work in design, so I sort of lost touch with things. While I was away, Alexis formed his band, and when I came back to England with Andy, I joined the band with Cyril Davies and Andy used to sing with us. We had some great guys in the band, like Jack Bruce. These guys knew what they were doing. I remember we were playing at a club in Ealing and Brian, Mick and Keith used to come along and sometimes sit in. It was a lot different then. People used to come up on the stand and have a go, and the whole thing was great.'

Charlie Robert Watts was born on 2 June 1941, the son of a lorry driver, Charles, and his wife, Lillian. He was brought up in London's King's Cross area, until moving to Wembley in 1952 and starting at the Tylers Croft Secondary School. Leaving school in 1957 with one 'O' level in art, he gained a place at the Harrow School of Art and eventually got a job with the advertising agency Hobson and Grey. By 1960 Watts, a sharp-suited Mod with an extraordinary knowledge of jazz and art, had immersed himself in London's coffee bar and jazz club scene. He joined Alexis Korner's Blues Incorporated in 1962 before moving on to Brian Knight's Blues By Six, and then the Stones.

Brian was very quick to let Charlie know that the Stones were without a drummer and in a fix.

1964 • Photo by Pictorial Press Ltd

CHAPTER 1

The Rise To Fame

Whatever the reasons behind Charlie Watts' joining the Stones, he set up his kit for his first gig with them on 14 January 1963 at the Flamingo Club in Soho. It was the beginning of a new year, and despite a lack of record company interest, the first two months were looking encouraging gig-wise. There was now a healthy list of dates coming up including a double return to the Marquee. Around this time, they became involved with a London club promoter called Giorgio Gomelski who was now running the Crawdaddy Club at the Station Hotel in Richmond. Giorgio was a large bearded 29-year-old of Franco-Russian descent whose involvement with music began during the 1950s, when he landed a job working for Chris Barber. From here he moved on to experiment with a crude early form of promotional video before turning finally to club management and ownership. In no time at all Gomelski had assumed an informal management role with the band. He began booking dates for them that finally included a Sunday night spot at his own Crawdaddy Club, and within a month he had taken the Stones from playing two nights a week to being a regular five-night-a-week attraction. All the gigs started to sell out. 'They took off in a fantastic way,' remembers Gomelski. 'Not so much because of the talent, but because of their determination to play a certain type of music. I knew less about the business of music, I only did it because I felt it was going to be a trend, and I felt that I could help this trend along. One of the very first things that got any interest at all in the Rolling Stones was a plan I had. In order to attract journalists, or indeed anyone, to my club I got some money together and spread the news that I was making a film in the hope that this would get the publicity thing going.'

He called a number of his friends who worked in music journalism, including Peter Jones, then editor of the pop weekly, *Record Mirror*. 'I had a call in the *Record Mirror* office from Giorgio, who insisted that I went down to see a band that he was featuring in a film on British rhythm and blues at Richmond, so I ended up down there, and it was the Rolling Stones. From that moment on, I became rather caught up in the Stones because the first thing that happened was I went in to listen to them working in what appeared to be a large unused saloon bar. There were cameras everywhere and Giorgio was doing his big film-directional bit, and Mick Jagger was acting as well as he could in the style that Giorgio wanted him to, but he looked pretty bored about the whole thing. It came to lunchtime, and there was a break, and I was introduced first to Brian Jones, and then to Mick Jagger.

Now what I'd seen had impressed me . . . largely because of the obvious animation of Jagger. I also think there was a fairly perfect foil in the guitar playing of Keith Richards, who didn't jump

about very much, and also in the rather soft and nice appearance of Brian. I did two things: I talked with a specialist writer on our paper called Norman Joplin, who really knew the rhythm and blues scene; and I insisted that he went to see them. He confirmed my roughly judged assessment of their musical ability and really liked them, so I gave him the freedom to write about them in the paper. This would be the first time that they'd had any press coverage.

'Mick and Brian had a big hang-up about making a record, so I said that the first thing they needed was a good manager. They didn't mention that anybody was acting as a manager for them, so I made a specific point of meeting up with Andrew Oldham. He was well known in the pop music industry because he was one of those on-the-fringe characters, determined to make a name for himself, and absolutely convinced that he was going to be a giant in the industry. There was one thing about Andrew which was that he was a tremendous worker and incredibly loyal to the artists he knew and believed in. For a while, he had worked as a part-time publicist for the then up-coming Beatles and I felt pretty sure that he would be the person to look after the Rolling Stones.'

Meanwhile, Giorgio's next logical step was to capture the sound of the Stones on a demo. He booked them into a studio in Portland Place, where they recorded five tracks in under three hours. They included Bo Diddley's 'Road Runner' and 'Diddley Daddy', Jimmy Reed's 'Honey, What's Wrong' and 'Bright Lights, Big City' and Muddy Waters's 'I Want To Be Loved'. Soon after, Gomelski started to tout the demos around London's record companies but to no avail. They were turned down flat by both EMI and Decca. EMI had already gone out on a limb with a new signing from Liverpool called the Beatles. Their first single, 'Love Me Do', was hardly setting the charts alight, therefore limiting the chances of EMI signing some more long-haired hopefuls.

Things changed very quickly for the Beatles. They had surpassed their somewhat unremarkable debut single by shooting straight to number 1 with their follow-up 'Please Please Me'. And they were about to appear live on a new pop music show called *Thank Your Lucky Stars*.

Gomelski brought the Beatles to the Crawdaddy Club from the television studios to see the Stones doing their set. He walked into the club half-way through and escorted all four Beatles to an exclusively reserved table by the side of the stage. The Stones had barely finished and thanked the sweating crowd before Giorgio frantically beckoned them over and introduced the two groups to each other. The Beatles were mid-way through a second tour of Great Britain and four days away from paying their first visit to the Royal Albert Hall, where a change of chart position and billing had put them as the headlining act topping the bill over American artists Chris Montez and Tommy Roe. The Beatles invited all six Stones along. Brian, Keith, Mick and Giorgio went along, while Bill, Charlie and Ian stayed home.

Arriving at the stage door of the Royal Albert Hall, the three Stones were greeted by a large crowd of hysterical girls who thundered towards them, clawing and grabbing at their hair as they mistook them for the Beatles. Safely inside, they decided this was what they really wanted.

By now, Peter Jones had met with Andrew Oldham, who decided to wander off to the Richmond to take a look for himself. 'It was a very rigid set up the first time I saw them,' remembers Andrew. 'They were very into the blues roots thing, but there was no production to the act at all. When I went down there, I was renting an office from a gentleman called Eric Easton and, as he was an agent, I tried to get him interested in the group. At the time he felt that the one member we should get rid of was Mick Jagger, because technically, "Mick Jagger could not sing"!'

Nevertheless, one half of the set was all Andrew had to see. He was completely bowled over by the band, and had already recognised their potential. During the interval, Oldham and Easton pushed their way through the crowd to reach Mick and asked if the band had a leader or manager, anyone they could talk to concerning business matters. Brian promptly spoke with them before resuming the stage, and the second half of their set. What Andrew did discover, however, was that although Gomelski looked out for the band, he was far from being considered their manager. The next day Oldham and Easton discussed the possibility of a joint management project concerning the Stones and asked Brian to come to their office in Regent Street to discuss some business, and, possibly, management matters. Brian jumped at the chance, but was careful to keep meeting hours late, going on to make a further four trips before admitting his interest. On his fifth visit to Oldham and Easton on 1 May 1963, Brian signed a three-year management contract on behalf of all six Stones.

In addition to the management contract, Brian struck a further private deal of his own. He secured with Oldham a separate contract that effectively entitled him to an extra £5 a week over and above anything the rest of the Stones would receive in the future, whether it be salary or otherwise. This was to cause a big internal bust-up for the Stones sooner rather than later.

Centre stage, Stones' manager, Andrew Loog Oldham • Photo by London Features International Ltd

It was at the Cavern Club in Liverpool some months later that Keith overheard Brian boasting to the manager of the club that he would soon be staying at better hotels than the others because he was the leader and made more money than the others.

Andrew, very aware of images, decided that he wanted to cut the group down to five and suggested that Ian would have to go altogether. In his mind he didn't look quite right – his appearance was all wrong for the band. 'Andrew was a publicity man,' recalled Ian. 'He was very conscious of producing a Beatles-type pop group, although without changing the music too much. He admitted that he knew nothing about music but wanted to cut the group down to five. I was much older than them. I did not like long hair, I never had my hair long.'

The idea that he should not be part of the group was a painful experience for Ian, although a little while later Andrew did come up with a compromise. Ian's departure from the band would only be for stage purposes. He would still be used on all future recordings as well as receiving a full sixth share in profits. 'I didn't really like the way Andrew steered the group,' Ian continues. 'In fact, if he'd just stuck to his publicity thing, which he was brilliant at, and kept his nose out of the music the band might have been better . . . although I do think he was very responsible for what they eventually achieved.'

Oldham's next item on the agenda was the insistence that Keith dropped the 's' from his surname in order to give a punchier ring to his name. More of a Cliff Richard overtone was needed, Oldham had decided.

Now the stage was set for the next inevitable problem – the return of Giorgio Gomelski, who had been away in Switzerland attending the funeral of his father. To explain all the recent developments, Brian introduced Andrew Oldham as an old school chum from Cheltenham. But Gomelski was astute enough to realise what had happened behind his back. He knew it was time to back out of the Stones. Like Ian, he was disgusted at Brian and Andrew's roughshod handling and insensitivity.

Andrew was now moving in on the Stones very quickly. After Brian had told him that the band had done some demos a few months before at the studios in Portland Place, Oldham and Easton quickly bought back the master, laying out over £100 in cash.

Oldham's next move was a brilliantly manoeuvred record deal with Decca, the company that had already passed on the band. Dick Rowe was Decca's A&R guy, at the time instantly famous as the man who turned down the Beatles. He had recently been a panelist alongside George Harrison at a music talent contest in Liverpool, where he had been told by George that he should check out a London band called the Rolling Stones. Not daring to make the same mistake twice, especially after being tipped off by a Beatle, he did just that. But Andrew exploited the embarrassed company man mercilessly. He had done his research and would only agree to a leasing deal with Decca, whereby he and Easton retained ownership of all recorded material by the band – a deal not even the Beatles had.

With the deal in the bag, the next step was to get the Stones back in the studio to cut a single. They used the huge Olympic Studios by the Thames for the first time on 10 May. Andrew was going to produce the record. 'He had the same naive experience or lack of experience that we had,' remembers Keith. 'When we made that first record, Andrew didn't know what he was doing in the studio; nor did we. We just learned as we went along. He relied on our experience of playing clubs for two years.'

The debut single 'Come On' was released 7 June 1963, and to coincide with its release Oldham lined up interviews with just about every teenage pop magazine that was being published, including *Rave, Fabulous, Beat* and *Sixteen*. The more serious music press, from *Melody Maker* to *Pop Weekly*, reviewed the single and voted it 'a miss'. And a miss it was . . . 'When we released that very first single we were doing gigs every night and we refused to play it,' recalled Keith. 'How could we go out and do our set of heavy rhythm and blues and then play this little pop song. It was too embarrassing.'

None of the Stones was particularly surprised at its poor chart performance; they had been most unenthusiastic about the finished result. 'As a first record, we knew that something like this was needed,' continues Keith. 'But we had no intention of that leading the way to what we were going to do next. We did "Come On" because it was the most commercial sound we were capable of making at the time, and the song had some kind of affinity with what we were used to doing.'

Around this time, the first journalist from a national newspaper did a piece on the group for the *Daily Mirror*. 'It was early in June 1963 when I was invited to go along to what was, in fact, one of my local pubs – the Station Hotel at Richmond,' recalled Patrick Doncaster. 'In the back room, there were possibly 500 people standing shoulder to shoulder in a place designed for maybe 100. The music was something that transformed everybody in that room as the people were carried away more than at a football match. They stood absolutely jammed together throwing each other to the ceiling, yelling 'yeah! yeah!' and they had an inch of floor to jump up and down from. It was like a ritual, tribal thing. I stood in the bar a little later and watched through a curtain, and a girl dashed out to this bar to ask the barman for a glass of water. When he gave it to her she poured it over her head, dashed back through the curtains into this mob of people and carried on jumping up and down. The barman turned to me and said, "That's all we got here sir; we don't serve any drinks, they all come out for water".'

Patrick's article was published on 13 June. The Rolling Stones could be just the thing that all the London-based national newspapers were looking for. 'The Beatles had just got away, and then came these five fantastic men producing something almost rivalling the Beatles in the south,' Patrick continues. 'I thought them sufficiently interesting and important to devote the lead of my column in the *Daily Mirror*. The headline on this particular piece read "TWITCHING THE NIGHT AWAY" because this was the only word I could think of that summed up the scene at the Station Hotel. There's quite an odd aftermath to this as well . . . When the directors of the company who owned the Station Hotel read my column, they rang up the hotel and said "Get rid of these guys, this is not the kind of publicity we want for our establishments".'

That was the bad news that Gomelski had in store for the Stones. There were to be no more gigs at the Richmond Crawdaddy Club as Ind Coope, the brewers, had ordered its immediate closure – the Crawdaddy, the Stones and Giorgio Gomelski were without a home. All was not lost, however, as Gomelski intended to relocate the Crawdaddy to the nearby Richmond Athletic Ground.

'There was a beautiful clubhouse on the ground,' remembers Harold Pendleton. 'Giorgio had applied to transfer his sessions with the Rolling Stones to this clubhouse, so I went guarantor for him because the secretary of the ground, a very nice chap called Commander Wheeler, said "Do you know this Gomelski character who looks like Rasputin who wants to take over the place?" I said yes, so he asked whether I would do business with him. I said "I wouldn't but I certainly recommend that you do, and I'll guarantee him because he's a very nice fellow". So Giorgio took over the clubhouse, and the Crawdaddy moved into there, and of course, they never looked back.'

The new Crawdaddy reopened on 30 June with an open-air gig that had the Stones topping the bill over Cyril Davies, Long John Baldry and a new group under Giorgio's wing called the Yardbirds, who featured a curious Brian Jones look-alike called Keith Relf, as well as a young guitarist named Eric Clapton.

Although the Stones had made their first television appearance some weeks earlier on the Birmingham-based show *Thank Your Lucky Stars* miming 'Come On', they had yet to appear live on radio. Back in January, Brian had sent a hand-written biography of the Stones to the BBC in the hope of getting an audition for the radio show *The Jazz Club*. Brian opened his letter with an introduction 'I am writing on behalf of the Rolling Stones rhythm and blues band. We have noticed recently in the musical press that you are seeking fresh talent for *Jazz Club*.' He went on to explain the band's make-up and influences and a full listing of venues they were playing: 'We have West End residencies at the Flamingo Jazz Club on Mondays, and at the Marquee Jazz Club on Thursdays, as well as several other suburban residencies. We already have a large following in the London area and in view of the vast increase of interest in rhythm and blues in Britain, an exceptionally good future has been predicted for us by many people. Our front line consists of vocal and harmonica electric, and two guitars supported by a rhythm section comprising bass, piano and drums. Our musical policy is simply to produce an authentic Chicago rhythm and blues sound using material of such R&B greats as Muddy Waters, Howlin' Wolf, Bo Diddley, Jimmy Reed and many others. We wonder if you could possibly arrange for us an audition.'

They got their audition on 23 April, but on 13 May, Brian received a rejection letter from the BBC that finished with 'We regret that the performance wasn't suitable for our purposes'. Since the audition, the Stones had signed a major record deal with Decca, and gained a new team of managers . . . *The Jazz Club* hardly seemed important.

In the meantime, Don Arden had lined up a pop package tour featuring Bo Diddley and the Everly Brothers. Eric Easton pulled a favour and managed to get the Stones on the bill as well, sharing third billing with Julie Grant, above the Flintstones and Mickie Most. It was a tremendous coup to appear on the same bill as acts of such stature – especially their own hero, Bo Diddley.

The tour opened on 29 September at the New Victoria Cinema in London, then hit the road to Birmingham, Wolverhampton, Liverpool, Sheffield and Manchester and further up to Scotland with two shows at the Odeon Theatre in Glasgow.

Mid-way through the tour the band started to rebel against Andrew, refusing to wear the stage outfits that Oldham had chosen for them. They consisted of cuban-heeled boots, black trousers and blue waistcoats topped with garish black and white check jackets. Oldham had quite unashamedly attempted to market the Stones as the natural successors to the Beatles in every way, and this included the band presentation of identical stage clothes.

It was ironic that the Stones' scruffy wild bunch image that was later exploited came about through something as simple as wanting to wear their own street clothes on stage and on television. 'The only time I asked them to compromise,' recalls Andrew, 'was with the first one or two records that we wanted to get on *Thank Your Lucky Stars*, where if they had turned up in their natural state they would never have gotten on. Then they were asked to wear uniforms of some description and they did, but once the position had changed to *Thank Your Lucky Stars* calling us to say can we have the Stones, they gradually started going on the way they felt like appearing.'

On 5 October 1963, the Stones finally appeared live on radio for *Saturday Club*. They performed a couple of Chuck Berry numbers, 'Memphis Tennessee' and 'Roll Over Beethoven'. Brian Matthew was the compere. 'I was so much older than they were, and therefore not really into this big rebellion thing which was their hallmark and continued to be so. Perhaps a little bit mistakenly, I found their attitude in the studio, as apart from their music, extremely truculent. One can now look back and see what they were all about, but here was the big establishment bit of the BBC and an aging disc jockey, and a load of – well you can imagine what Jagger would have called it – and I don't think there was a very good personal relationship . . . at least I didn't think so at the time. In those days we always had to interview the groups, and this didn't go down at all well because one got no answer, which is an interviewer's death. I really didn't like them much at all, though this had nothing to do with their music, which was something apart. It was odd that many years later I had a letter from Brian Jones' mother – a query in connection with another programme that I was doing – and she said "I felt I could write to you, and you would be sympathetic in this, because Brian always used to say how much he liked you, and how well you got on". I felt about as big as a pea. It was ludicrous. It was very difficult unless you were of an age with the Stones, and into what they were doing; you couldn't really have any kind of close relationship.'

The time was now approaching for the follow-up single to 'Come On'. For weeks the band had been rehearsing whenever possible between gigs. A shortlist was drawn up of songs that could be recorded as cover versions. There were things like 'Fortune Teller' and 'Poison Ivy' but these were thought to be too well known. A couple of sessions, one at Decca's West Hampstead studios and another at Studio 51 in Newport Street did not provide the right formula. Now frustrated and exhausted with non-productive tension, Andrew left the studio and paced through Soho attempting to find inspiration. He finally found it in the Beatles. John Lennon and Paul McCartney were leaving a Variety Club awards presentation in Jermyn Street when Andrew greeted them with his problem. Lennon offered a simple but generous solution – he said the Stones could record a number they had written for their forthcoming album. Oldham rushed the two Beatles back to the studio where the song was put down in one take after a quick run through. A Beatles song done in the Rolling Stones style just could not fai – and fail it did not. 'I Wanna Be Your Man', released on 1 November went straight into the Top Ten.

As the Stones continued to play daily gigs up until the end of 1963 with only one day off on Boxing Day, Keith reflected on the previous winter. 'It's ingrained on me. Luckily, we had nothing else to do, and we were pretty determined. There was no other way for it to go except up since we were determined that we were going to stick together and play. We were down to thieving potatoes out of supermarkets and selling beer bottles back to the off-licence anyway, so there was nothing else to do except push on. It had to get better even if it didn't get fantastic. It was difficult, but it was fun too.'

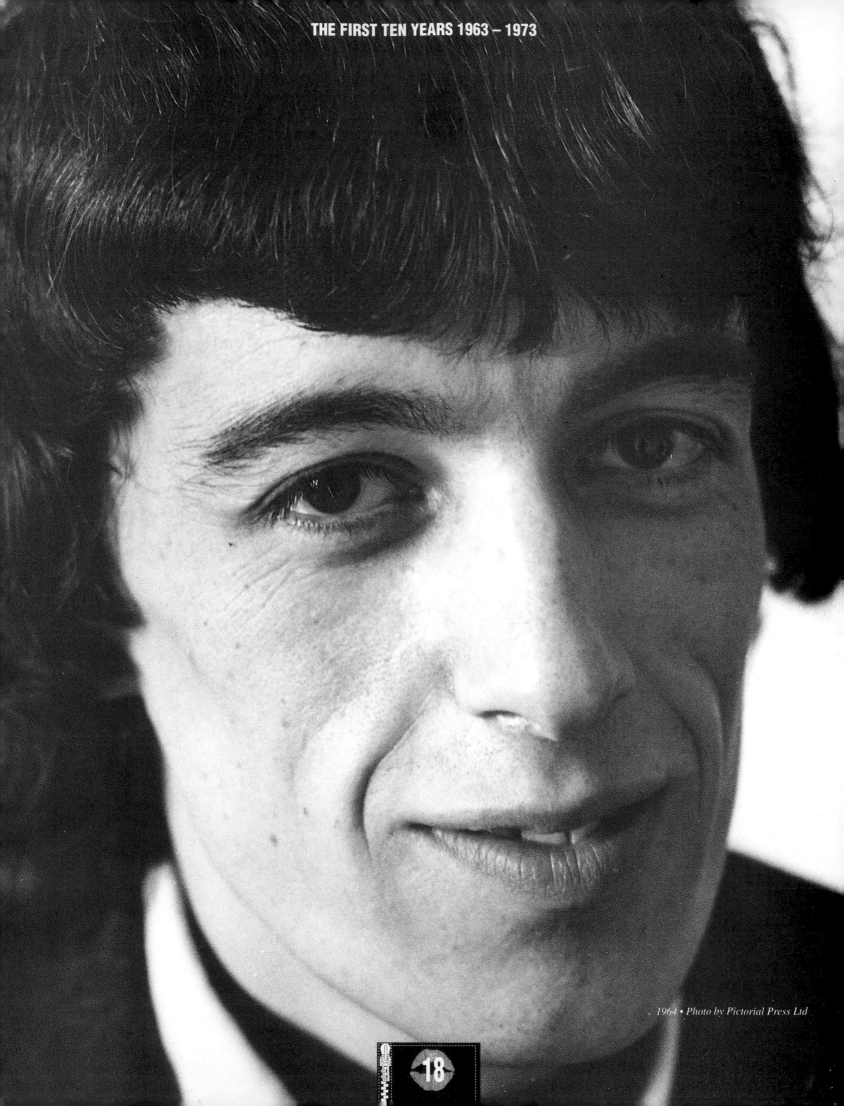

1964 • Photo by Pictorial Press Ltd

CHAPTER 2

Would You Let Your Daughter Marry A Rolling Stone?

The Stones kicked straight into the first day of 1964 with an appearance on the very first edition of the new BBC pop show *Top Of The Pops* before embarking on their second nationwide tour of Great Britain two days later. On this outing, the Stones shared top billing with Phil Spector's all-girl American group the Ronettes. The endless round of Odeon Theatres and ballroom appearances continued at a relentless pace for the next few months, with barely two days off in a row. There were two shows a night; each one as frantic as the one before. It was a fearsome pace that did not let up as their first album was released.

The Rolling Stones shot straight to number 1, with a cover featuring a dark and moody close-up portrait of the group by the aspiring young photographer David Bailey. The white-bordered photograph on the sleeve had no graphics or title except the Decca record company logo in the top right-hand corner. This was a risky and pioneering step on the part of Decca, implying that the Rolling Stones themselves were bigger than their music.

'That entire record,' remembers Keith, 'was virtually our stage act apart from one or two dubs thrown in. Most of it was straight from what we had played at Studio 51 or Richmond, but when we recorded it we did it on a two-track Revox in a room insulated with egg cartons at Regent Sound. Under those primitive conditions it was very easy to make that kind of sound.'

It was also single time again. Oldham realised that if the success was to continue, they needed a healthy shot of commercialism in their choice of recording material. He also realised that the Lennon – McCartney song-writing set-up had taken the Beatles to new heights of acceptance and success, and he set about developing an enforced song-writing partnership for Jagger and Richards.

'I suppose the credit for that really must go to Andrew,' recalls Keith, 'because I never thought of writing . . . it never occurred to me. I thought that was something else. It was like being a novelist, or it was like being a computer operator for all I knew. It was just a completely different field that I hadn't thought of. I thought of myself solely as a guitar player, and Mick hadn't thought of it either. I suppose we dabbled with it occasionally when we were sitting around with Brian. I remember a couple of times we just gave up in despair. It was really Andrew who forced us to sit down and try it and got us through that initial period which you have to go through writing. You just write absolute rubbish – things you've heard, rewrites of other people's songs – until you start coming out with songs of your own, and it was Andrew who really made us persevere with that.'

Oldham knew that establishing the song-writing element within the band was essential. In fact, it was now the main objective. The band needed good, commercially viable pop songs. It would be seen as a complete turnaround from the earthy Chicago Blues sound that had given rise to the band's early popularity.

'That period, if you remember rightly, which I very rarely do,' says Mick, 'everyone used to re do hits that were like standards. For instance "Money", "Some Other Guy", that was a good one, "Mashed Potato" . . . But then you start to get the feeling that you had to write your own because you're running out of them, so we just started writing. We never really wrote any blues numbers to start off with. The things we wrote were more like ballads or pop songs. That style came more naturally to us than writing original blues, which is very difficult to write actually. Even now, good original blues is difficult to write . . . ask any blues singer, whatever colour, it just is! Writing pop songs is where we started. The first song we ever wrote was called "It Should Be You", I think.'

Top Of The Pops, 1964 • Photo by Pictorial Press Ltd

A newly signed Decca singing hopeful named George Bean covered that first song. Both song and artist were never heard of again.

In the meantime Oldham, determined to expand his publishing operation, offered another Jagger – Richards song to Gene Pitney as a future new single. 'I guess it was just prior to '24 Hours From Tulsa',' recalls Gene. 'Andrew was my publicist and was managing the Rolling Stones, and having him as my publicist, we got to meet each other. I recorded a song of theirs called "That Girl Belongs To Yesterday", but it's funny because they wrote it their own way, and it was probably a perfect opportunity for a winner song; but I changed the whole thing because it wasn't, or they weren't, right for the market at that time: the market hadn't changed yet. I put it into more of a ballad-type thing, more like my type of material, and I recorded that in the studio. Mick and Keith and everybody was there!

'I guess the funniest thing that ever happened with regard to the Stones was when I stopped in from Paris one time when Phil Spector was also in London. Andrew called me at the hotel and said he was having a terrible time because they were trying to do the follow-up to "I Wanna Be Your Man" and all the boys hated each other that day. They got them in the studio – a little dinky studio in Denmark Street – and he couldn't get them to do anything. I had five bottles of cognac that I was bringing home, so I took a bottle over to the studio and told them it was my birthday and that it was a custom in my family that when anybody had a birthday, everybody had to drink a glass of cognac until the bottle was empty. So we ended up with a hell of a session. I played piano on the date, and Phil Spector played an empty cognac bottle with a half dollar, clicking it, and we played on the B-side, which was "Little By Little".'

'Little By Little' first appeared on the B-side of their third single 'Not Fade Away', but later as one of the twelve tracks on their first album that came out on 29 May. Three days after the album's release, the Stones flew to America for a whistle-stop promotional tour. 'When I met them, nobody had really heard of them anywhere, not even in England, and certainly not the rest of the world,' continues Gene. 'I was surprised when I met them only because of the hair, and the appearance. I remember I had a fellow with me who was in the Senate in the state of Connecticut. We took a picture of the boys with their arms around him, and when he got home, his wife asked him who the ugly women were with their arms around him. That's how uneducated the public was, especially the American public, to that long hair and that type of look at that time.'

But, strangely enough, it was not the hair, the look, or even the music that would send shockwaves throughout the States. Music journalist Judy Sims observed that they were 'dangerous and likely to corrupt the American youth. They have that outlaw charm as if they're taking it one step further . . . even in their stage show, it always seems as if Jagger is trying to outrage'. Being in the States, the Stones could hardly pass up the opportunity to record their first US studio session at Chess in Chicago, the home of so many of their musical heroes.

'The first time I met them was sort of out of a clear blue sky,' remembers sound engineer, Ron Malo. 'Marshall Chess had met the Stones in London and had invited them to come over and record in our studios. They were young, exciting people. When they came in we had a lot of fun together. They were very co-operative and it was an exciting thing to be with them, except they spent hours and hours playing along with the old Chess records and learning all of the licks so that they had that feeling.

'They learnt by the old Chess records, and to be able to record at the Chess studios was, I guess, a great thing for them. They wanted that hard close American sound, and it's strange because they came over and I set up the studio exactly the same as I would have for any of the dates I had been doing at that time. After the first run through, and the first tune, everybody in the control room said, "that's the sound we've been looking for", and I really enjoyed recording them. I didn't have to work to get a sound. It was very simple to set up, very simple microphoning. The first song we did, to the best of my knowledge, was "It's All Over Now". It was the first song we recorded and, as it turned out, their first American hit record. We did two takes on it. They did one take, and we had some problems in the performance that wanted a little change because it wasn't quite right. We did another take and that was it. I remember on that first session, we did thirteen tunes in one day, or one night, as it was actually. They came in, we started in the afternoon and worked all night, finishing early in the morning. We did thirteen tunes complete, mixed, done, ready to be mastered . . . and that for a group is totally amazing. We were used to it at Chess, though . . . we often cut LPs in four, five, six hours. With Muddy Waters or Sonny Boy Williamson, we'd cut the whole LP in one afternoon.

'The tune "2120 South Michigan Avenue" was a sort of tongue-in-cheek thing that they did in a hurry because Muddy Waters stopped by at the studio and they really enjoyed that. They wanted to know when so and so was coming by, or when Buddy Guy was going to be there, or Willie Dixon, or Chuck Berry. So Muddy came in and they did a couple of his things. Then they did this tune they wanted to dedicate to Muddy and, for want of a better title, the tune became "2120 South Michigan Avenue – Muddy Waters Was There". When I saw the tune come out with "2120 South Michigan Avenue" which was the studio address, it was kind of cute, and Muddy got a big kick out of that, but the "Muddy Waters Was There" part of it was deleted somewhere along the line.'

Classic 1964 shot supplied to US magazines emphasising the group's London origins
Photo by Pictorial Press Ltd

On returning to England, the Stones found themselves voted second to the Beatles in the *Record Mirror* Pop Poll under the World Male Vocal Group section, and first in the British category. Their album was still at number 1, and so was the EP of the same name. Their next single, 'It's All Over Now', was due for release on 26 June and they were about to create more controversy the following day when they appeared on *Juke Box Jury* to vote the latest record releases a 'hit' or a 'miss'.

'It was rather extraordinary because it was during their most rebellious time, when they wanted particularly to knock the establishment and *Juke Box Jury* and perhaps myself,' recalls the programme's compere, David Jacobs. 'We were very much part of the established record scene, you see. We had a small rehearsal and they were put in their places at the desk, and when I came on stage, they lolled about on purpose except, strangely enough, Brian Jones, who for some strange reason got up, put his hand out, and said "Good afternoon sir." It was quite a startling moment . . . I didn't expect him to do that, and the other boys looked very embarrassed. But we went on to do the programme, and I'm sorry to say that what they did was particularly good for themselves, and maybe not too bad for the programme, but it seemed a bit silly, because they appeared to be five ignorant, moronic imbeciles. They went out of their way to utter grunts and groans, and not be able to put two words together, whereas we all know that they're a very articulate bunch, and it seemed a pity that they did it on purpose. They didn't do the show any harm and got themselves a lot of publicity and they used it as a vehicle not for anything other than promoting themselves.'

The Stones later claimed that they were just being themselves, 'If stupid and corny records are included then that's hard luck. We're just not the sort of blokes to get mealy-mouthed just to say polite things for the sake of saying them,' retorted Brian.

The furore of this television appearance had hardly been forgotten when they returned to the front pages of the national press on 25 July. While appearing at the Empress Ballroom in Blackpool a riot broke out resulting in the Stones bolting from the stage for their own safety. Mick told BBC reporter Tom Jermans that the trouble developed during their second show. 'We could almost see it building up, this tension. All these thugs were getting drunker and drunker and more violent. There weren't more than twenty that started it off, and they just pushed their way to the front. They were pushing girls out the way, and in doing it, I saw some girls who were punched and kneed in the stomach. It was really violent and horrible – I've never seen anything like it – and then we were pulled off and it just got madder and madder. Our equipment got smashed up too.'

While not every concert finished in chaos like the one in Blackpool, they always came close to it. Two hundred fans fainted at the concert at Lord Bath's Longleat House, two policewomen fainted at the Belle Vue in Manchester when they and fifty other policemen tried to control 3,000 screaming teenagers, and Rex, the police dog, had to be led away for rest after twenty minutes of screaming by 7,000 fans at the Isle of Man show.

'They were the most exciting groups, them and the Beatles,' said Jimmy Saville. 'The Beatles were exciting because they just generated excitement, but the Stones were exciting because they generated the excitement plus they did a bit of leaping about as well. The Beatles never leapt about, but the Stones did . . . they always used to have a bit of jump up and down. Mick was whirling like a Dervish the whole time, and that was a tremendous communicator of excitement. At one big function that I was at with them, the promoters paid me a huge sum of money to introduce the Stones, but such was the incredible sound from the audience that I rushed on to the stage and I never said a word. All I did was take a leaf out of their book and sprang in the air, and waved my arms about, and kept pointing off stage and miming as if I was playing a guitar, and never uttered a sound. The screams built up to the most incredible pitch, and all of a sudden I jumped up and down like a orang-utan and beckoned the lads. They came running on stage and, as they passed, they said to me "What a bloody way to earn a living you have" . . . I was the only compere that didn't open his mouth.'

The Stones at Longleat, 1964 • Photo by Popperfoto

To channel all this enthusiasm and mania, Andrew launched the official fan club with Shirley Arnold, the Stones' secretary, running the operation. 'At that time, it was crazy. The fan club was storming. We had a post office van come round every morning to deliver the mail – sacks and sacks of it. Birthday presents, presents from all over the world, which were incredible. When I think back now about the money those kids spent on things like lighters, you know, really good things. In one week we had 1,000 applications to join the fan club, and we used to sit in the office to 10, 12, 2 in the morning. The fan club itself was 5 shillings a year subscription, and we wrote to all the kids. I did the English part of the club, and there was another girl doing the foreign part. It was just crazy.'

Meanwhile, plans for the Stones' second (and first major) tour of the USA had been underway for some time. Their first album had been released there under the slogan 'England's newest hit makers' and reached the number 11 spot in the US Top Twenty.

They flew straight to New York and played two shows at the Academy of Music, followed by an appearance on the massively popular *Ed Sullivan Show*. As the Stones played, the live audience got carried away and invaded the stage, intent on tearing it down for souvenirs. Pandemonium ensued.

They crossed the States playing fifteen shows in twenty-one days, as well as incorporating another studio session at Chess.

'We had no security,' recalls Ron Malo. 'The way the building was situated, it was assumed that we wouldn't have any fans outside, but as it turned out we would have half a dozen or a dozen teenagers standing outside the window. At Chess at that time, the studios and control room were on the second floor, and the control room had just a little louvred window at the back which looked down at the sidewalk. These girls would be out there with their little home tape recorders pointing them up to the window, and we'd finish a take, and you'd hear applause going on from outside and the guys would wave down to them, or yell at them, and they'd say "where's Mick?", or "Where's so and so?". They wanted to talk to them. We couldn't get rid of them because we were working all night, so we would have to call the police, only if for the girls' protection. They'd come over and advise them to leave because the neighbourhood wasn't too safe for them to be out there.

'There was another time, when we went over to have lunch at the Bats Restaurant. The studio was right across from the hotel where Al Capone had his offices, and the restaurant was downstairs. We went in at the back door, and I asked the owner of the restaurant, Nick Bat, if there was a place in the back dining room that I could put the fellas in. I told him they were famous recording artists and they would just as soon be out of the regular restaurant; but you can't keep a secret from anybody. Now the restaurant owner's relatives, children, or whoever were coming back. "Can we get their autographs?" or something like that. So now we have another thing going completely with the fans.'

The Stones then played six shows in California supported by the Byrds. The energy of these shows was amazing; the hysteria of the audience, the sheer police presence and security people. It was madness and the authorities didn't know how to handle it at all. The things that some of the girls threw on stage were also amazing . . . panties and bras with messages and invitations, or offers of an extremely rude nature by the sweetest of young girls. Brian loved the tours and went completely overboard.

'Everybody went through their star trip,' recalls Keith, 'but I think Brian was the only one that it changed in a really deep way, and probably not for the better. He couldn't cope with it really, and it did change him almost immediately. It was very difficult for him, and not made any easier by the rest of us, because nobody had the time to look after somebody else. It's like some platoon going off to recce your enemy positions or something. You get there and it's every man for himself because you've got your own trips you're going through. And on top of that you're working every night, and if you're not working, you're recording, and when that's going on for two or three years non-stop, it's all you can do just to keep yourself going, and to keep yourself standing up. To look after another cat is just impossible, and that's one of the sadder things about stardom. When it happens that fast, especially if you're in a group of people, if one of them isn't quite strong enough to deal with that situation, there's very little you can do to help him.'

The furious pace that the Stones were now keeping made little allowance for a private life. Their itinerary was running a good six months ahead of them, with two shows a night being commonplace and as many radio or television appearances a day.

By now, Oldham's mania for publicity seemed detrimental to the band; he would always publicise even the most trivial incidents. 'Stories were planted with different journalists and they were often exaggerated,' remembers Peter Jones. 'I spent quite a few days on tour with the Rolling Stones, and I didn't find them half as outlandish as some papers did. I think stories were created quite deliberately in order to nurture an image.'

'They are called the ugliest group in Britain,' reported the *Daily Mirror*. 'They are not looked on very kindly by most parents or by adults in general. They are even used in the type of article that asks big brother if he would let his sister go out with one of them!'

But there was one bright note amongst this combined negativity. An article written by Jimmy Saville appeared in *The People* which read: 'They're clean guys, it's just that the world wants to inflict on them an image of dirt and this, that and the other. For instance, I was on a gig with them in a place in Lancashire and we were all marooned, the six of us in a dressing room, and it looked like we were going to be there for three or four hours. A lovely little old lady came in and said she'd "organised some tea and sandwiches", and I thanked her. Then one of the lads, I think it was Keith, put his arm around her shoulder and said "That's very nice of you to think of us", and she says "Take your filthy hands off me!" I was most upset at that because they really are nice lads, and this image had been inflicted on them that they were supposed to be dirty. This lady had fixed us up with the tea and as soon as he'd tried to be nice, which was his nature, she'd jumped on to this image. It upset me for ages, and I carried it about in my mind as an example of how the world can be wrong by being influenced by the media.'

As rumours started circulating that all was not well within the Stones' camp, their new single, 'It's All Over Now', was released, entering the chart at number 7, and number 1 a week later. 'I don't care a damn if our new record has reached number 1,' said a rebellious Jagger. 'What's it matter anyway? "It's All Over Now" has reached the top; that's great, but none of us have been worrying about it.'

By now, the Stones were on yet another nationwide tour of Great Britain in support of their hit single and just-released EP 'Five By Five'. The tour, like the others before, was set at such a relentless pace that they probably did not notice how each show became more and more riot prone. 'When you're on stage, you're so conscious of it that you try to forget everything else and just concentrate on playing,' remarked Keith. 'You try to ignore the audience as much as possible. If you think too much about the audience you will just dry up and paralyse yourself.'

On this tour the hotels they stayed at were being besieged by the fans days before their arrival. They would now leave by a back entrance and dart straight into Ian's van, which seemed to go miraculously unnoticed. To avoid the gathered mob at each gig they backed the van right up to the stage doors. There was always a sigh of relief once inside the safety of the dressing room, though they were unaware that outside the fans would be taking wing mirrors, aerials and door handles from the van. There was even one occasion when a tyre went missing, so from then on, Ian would always stay with the van during the Stones' two performances.

After the tour, and without telling the rest of the Stones, Charlie married a girl called Shirley Ann Shepherd on 14 October at Bradford Register Office in Yorkshire.

The next single, their fourth, shot straight to number 1. 'Little Red Rooster' was another blues number that had originally been recorded by Willie Dixon. The Stones were now like the biggest band there was: bigger than The Beatles in a sense because the Beatles were establishment while the Stones were the most rebellious, the most exciting, raunchy, dangerous band there was. They were now on what seemed like an unstoppable crest of a wave.

The Stones on 'Ready Steady Go' • Photo by London Features International Ltd

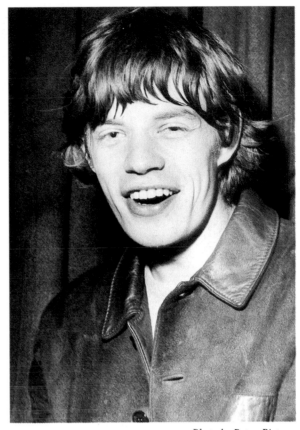

Photo by Retna Pictures

Photo by Rex Features

Poster for New Brighton Tower,
Merseyside, 1963 • Photo by Pictorial Press Ltd

'Top Of Th[e

On 'The Ed Sullivan Show', USA • Photo by Range Pictures Ltd

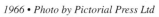
1966 • Photo by Pictorial Press Ltd

Photo by Pictorial Press Ltd

Rock 'n' Roll Circus Invitation, 1968 • Supplied by Kay Rowley

*You are invited to the
Rolling Stones' Rock and Roll Circus
on Wednesday, 11th December, 1968
at the studios of Intertel Television,
Wycombe Road, Wembley, Middlesex.
Nearest tube: Stonebridge Park .
(Bakerloo line)*

*18.30 – 23.00
Costumes Provided*

I realise and agree that you are the rightful owners of the copyright of the film - 'THE ROLLING STONES' ROCK AND ROLL CIRCUS' - in which I am to take part in consideration of entrance to the recording.

I further agree that you, or any persons authorized either directly or indirectly by you, are at liberty to use the film exposed and any reproductions or adaptions of either complete or any part for commercial or private usage.

Signed

Photo by Retna Pictures

Mick with Marianne Faithful • Photo by London Features International Ltd

Ex-Yardbirds guitarist Mick Taylor replaces Brian Jones, June 1969 • Photo by Retna Pictures

Hyde Park, 1969 • Photo by Pictorial Press Ltd

Mick and Bill with director Jean-Luc Godard on the set of the film 'Sympathy For The Devil', 1968 Photo by Pictorial Press Ltd

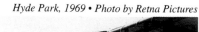

Hyde Park, 1969 • Photo by Retna Pictures

Hyde Park, 1969 • Photo by London Features International Ltd

CHAPTER 3

The Weekend Starts Here

he Stones began the new year with a short series of gigs in Ireland, followed by their first tour of Australia and New Zealand sharing the bill with Roy Orbison. As they arrived at Sydney airport on 21 January 1964, 3,000 fans rioted and 300 girls tore through a chain wire fence smashing their way into the quarantine area. The fans were very passionate, and Mick was a master at whipping them up so there was a tremendous tension and the band exploited it brilliantly. Everyone wanted to make sure they toured there again and again. By now, the Stones realised they were going to be very big – possibly even bigger than the Beatles.

Only six days earlier, their second album had shot straight to the number 1 spot in the UK charts. *'The Rolling Stones No. 2'* again featured a dark and moody close-up portrait. The cover again bore the white-bordered photograph with no graphics or title, just the Decca record company logo which this time had been moved to the bottom right-hand corner. The message was the same: the Rolling Stones themselves were bigger than their music.

In the meantime, the fifth single was being planned for release on 26 February. It would be the first to have a Jagger – Richard composition as the A-side. 'The Last Time' had gone to number 1 as they arrived back in Great Britain for another nationwide tour topping the bill over the Hollies, Dave Berry, the Checkmates and Goldie and the Gingerbreads. The compere was Johnny Ball.

'It was opening night at Edmonton, and there were crowds outside the theatre and in the car park,' remembers Johnny. 'We were all worried about the cars getting scratched. The show started and was going quite well until Goldie and the Gingerbreads went on, when we all realised that the Stones hadn't yet arrived. I remember Eric Easton told me to get out there and hold the audience until they got there, so I rushed out and, of course, there was no-one left on the bill. It had to be the Stones next so the fans were going wild. There weren't many people sitting down, most of them crowded down the front and were hanging off the circle. I did a few gags and surprisingly got smiles and titters, but soon the chanting "We want the Stones" started! I conducted them until it speeded up and petered out, and as soon as it did, I tried three more gags, but then the chanting started again. Every time they cheered and shouted I took a bow although they were cheering and shouting at me. Then I got weary and a little bit scared because I realised I couldn't go on much longer, so I sat down cross-legged and Dave Berry's group started bringing on Coca-Cola and packets of crisps. I went through this eating and drinking and every time the chanting started I speeded it up until it petered out again, and then sat down again, and so on. Eventually I got the word that they'd arrived and to keep going for another five minutes. Once I knew the end was in sight, I carried on extremely relieved!

'The whole tour was very hectic. I remember in Manchester, it was horrifying when the bouncers lost their grip and there were dozens of girls on stage, and falling into the orchestra pit. A girl broke her ankle and the St John's Ambulance people dragged her out to the foyer and sat her down, but when they turned to the phone, she'd gone back in! No-one heard a thing I was saying for two weeks, but it was great training, after that I could work anything, absolutely anything.'

The Stones were, by now, on a prolific run and enjoying constant success. They had scored two number 1 singles and two number 1 albums in a matter of months and sold out every show on both sides of the Atlantic. When they played the London Palladium in the summer, the two shows incited scenes of mass hysteria and the biggest police presence they had yet encountered, and as they flew out to West Germany on 20 August o play a short series of gigs, their sixth single was released. '(I Can't Get No) Satisfaction' would become the most distinctive Stones hit, yet Keith never thought of it as single material. 'The first time I think I heard it was when Keith was playing around with a riff in Clearwater, Florida,' remembers Mick, 'and the funny thing about it was that he only had the first bit, and then he had a riff, but it sounded like a country thing on an acoustic guitar . . . not at all like rock. But he didn't really like it; he thought it was a joke, not a single or anything, so I just wrote the verses and the "hey hey" and all that.'

It was while they were playing those gigs in Germany that Brian was introduced to a young German – Italian model called Anita Pallenberg, a stunningly beautiful 19-year-old. Brian fell for her instantly. 'I decided to kidnap Brian,' stated Anita. 'It sounds ridiculous, but they even made a film about it, about kidnapping a pop star. It was called *Privilege* and starred Paul Jones. This was the original story. Brian seemed to be the most sexually flexible. I knew I could just talk to him. As a matter of fact, when I met him I was his groupie really. I got backstage with a photographer; I told him I just wanted to meet them.'

Brian very quickly threw himself head-first into a relationship with Anita and for the next few months they would hop about Europe as well as meeting up at every Stones gig. Brian was the most popular Stone at this time, and he also had the most stunning girlfriend, but that would all change in due course.

Big Beat
Festival
of 1964

A NIGHT
WITH THE
STARS

at
THE ROYAL
ALBERT HALL

(Manager:
C. R. Hopper)

STARRING

BRIAN POOLE
AND THE
TREMELOES

DUSTY
SPRINGFIELD
AND THE ECHOES

THE ROLLING
STONES

THE SWINGING
BLUE JEANS

and full supporting
cast

(artistes arranged in
alphabetical order)

SATURDAY ,
FEBRUARY 1,

The weekend still started with *Ready Steady Go* and Cathy McGowan. 'We'd no idea that they'd become that big because after seeing them for so long they were like anybody who worked in the building, but the reaction to me talking to Mick, or dancing with him or anything like that was terrible,' recalls Cathy. 'I was called everything for that, terrible letters and abuse. Then there were other letters that asked how could I bear to dance with anybody who looked like that, or sit next to them, and that they were just dirty. They looked dead rough, but of course they weren't, that was just the way they were. Whenever we wanted them, if we said we were doing the New Year's Eve show, Christmas Eve, anything, they were always there. They would always make a special thing to come to *Ready Steady Go*. I remember when we went to Switzerland to do the programme, the Swiss television people said they would only be interested if we could bring somebody of such importance that it would be worth their while setting it all up for us, so the Stones came with us. Another time when we did a show from Paris and had taken the Who, I told Mick before that I was worried sick because the Who were not like the Rolling Stones: if they decided to co-operate one minute they would, but if they decided it wasn't their day they wouldn't. I thought it would be a disaster because I couldn't speak French, and wouldn't be allowed to go again, but Mick turned up to give us support, to be a star. If anything went wrong, at least everyone would want to watch Mick Jagger in Paris, and so he just came along.

June 1964, at Andrew Oldham's apartment block office, London • Photo by Pictorial Press Ltd

They had also released their third album *Out Of Our Heads* which entered the charts at number 3. This was the first album to feature graphics and title on the jacket, though it still retained the white-bordered black-and-white photograph image.

From the dates in England, the tour moved on to West Germany for a short series of gigs before the band flew out to Canada for the start of a mammoth US tour that would take them up to New Year's Eve and *Ready Steady Go*. 'It was the best rock television show ever, anywhere, because it was years ahead of its time, and had a very good feeling in the room,' Mick remembers. 'We used to play live, but only after two days' sound check. The first day was just the sound check, the second day was sound and camera check. I'm only talking about ten minutes, but that's not just walking in there and ripping off a couple of numbers. I think with live TV, the camera people have got to know, the sound people have got to know, everyone's got to know! It's got to be walked through; it's TV, it's like rehearsing for a show. It's a three-day job. You could be spontaneous within what you'd rehearsed because you were so well rehearsed that everyone knew what was going to happen, so that if you just moved off it slightly, you were followed. It was a good TV show.'

The director of *Ready Steady Go* was Michael Lindsey-Hogg, who really did more for the Stones on television than anybody else. He was basically a Stones freak. He had worked on the programme for the last eighteen months, and had developed a technique where the visual is frozen, but the music continues. It took a lot of work and a lot of rehearsal, but the Stones were very good at that sort of thing. Once Michael had explained to Mick what his idea was, everyone associated with the programme, including the band, was in the studios for two or three hours' extra rehearsals to work out the technical problems.

During rehearsals at 'Ready Steady Go' studios • Photo by London Features International Ltd

CHAPTER 4

The Nature Of Their Game

For 1966, the Stones released their fourth album, and their first completely self-penned LP. It was titled *Aftermath* and inevitably went straight to number 1. The album's fourteen tracks bore song-writing credits for Mick and Keith, and much-publicised praise for Brian's musical integrity and instrumental supremacy. His range included everything from the conventional to the exotic and the downright ridiculous. Harpsichord, dulcimer, sitar and marimbas as well as a child's plastic banjo were all incorporated brilliantly and innovatively into the music.

Peter Jones reviewed the album in *Record Mirror* saying that 'Brian started out as a much better guitarist than Keith, but Keith had more of a natural feel, whereas Brian was capable of getting exactly the same sound and feel he wanted out of any instrument. "Paint It Black" was an obvious example. Brian played the sitar like he played rhythm guitar. It probably made George Harrison cringe, but it worked brilliantly.'

Keith Altham, who was writing for the *New Musical Express* during the making of *Aftermath*, interviewed Brian several times, and concluded: 'It was almost a natural feel he had for picking up instruments and playing them immediately, but he was limited in what he could do. As soon as he found out he could play a few bits and pieces on it he didn't have the discipline or the concentration to stick at it and take it any further. Just like the latest plaything – pick it up, play it, put it down and forget it – which was a bit like how he was with people.'

Even though the album bore original song-writing credits for Jagger and Richards, and some were even covered by other artists, there did not appear to be the rush to get to the songs as there would be with a new Beatles album. Groups were now invariably recording their own compositions on records and as such changed the role of the music publisher, who up to this time had been solely responsible for finding new songs for their artist to record. 'The change was really in the role the publisher plays in regards to the promotion of the material,' explained David Platts, then head of Essex Music, the parent company of the Stones' music-publishing interests. 'And also in the amount of royalties received by the writers.

Brian Jones complete with sitar • Photo by Pictorial Press Ltd

Under normal circumstances this would have been an equal division between the composer and the publisher, but what really happened with the Stones was that we took on more of a role as a protector and a policeman, I suppose, in order to protect their rights and to make sure that their royalties were correctly collected and correctly accounted for. Publishing has changed from being 50/50 to a situation whereby the artists, who by and large are the writers as well, have the larger share of royalties on records that they originate, and the publisher has the right to maybe better terms when he gets other artists to record the material. It is probably not known that many of the songs that are successful here and in America are recorded in Europe by European artists in the local language, and that's really where our job is. Quite a few songs going back to the early days were covered by other artists, some American of course, and I suppose the big songs like "Satisfaction" which are what we call a standard do continue to be recorded by all sorts of people and do develop.'

By 1973, there would be over fifty versions of 'Satisfaction' recorded by other artists. 'My favourite cover version,' says Mick, 'is "Sympathy For The Devil" done as a spoken narration. It sounds like an actor but I don't know who it is. I also like Marianne's version of "As Tears Go By".'

'Probably some of the covers of "Satisfaction" are among my favourites,' reflects Keith. 'Otis's (Redding) version really knocked me out and Aretha's (Franklin) version was really great. As for writing things for other people, most of them were jokes, like the Gene Pitney thing, and Marianne Faithfull. It was really tongue-in-cheek stuff. We didn't do much for other people really. I can only think of three records: the Chris Farlowe one, and the Gene Pitney one, and Marianne's first record. They're the only three that stick in my mind as having been written for other people.'

By now, Andrew had set up his own record label, Immediate Records. Many thought he was following in the same footsteps as Phil Spector. 'The main factor of forming Immediate Records was to beat the four record-company system which was Pye, Phillips, Decca and EMI, and prove that an independent could win. I have to hand the thanks for the formula to Spector, who in '61 and '62 proved that he could do it in Americ;, but you could say that I was out to beat exactly the same system in England. As the first record we had went to number 1, we definitely proved it.'

Although that first number 1 hit for Andrew's label was of American origin, Oldham wanted to develop and promote British artists. 'I used to do the Ricky Tic Club and Reading Town Hall,' remembers Chris Farlowe. 'Then I joined an organisation called the Gummel Brothers who were running all the rhythm and blues clubs everywhere, and all the artists as well. They were the main men and they told me that Andrew Oldham had got a new label starting, called Immediate, and asked if I'd like to be on it. I said yes because it sounded like a good deal as they were young and knew what to do, or so we thought. So they signed me to Andrew, and I went up to see him and Mick. That was when Mick was living at Harley House in Marylebone Road. They played me a track called 'Kink', I believe it was, and that was my first recording with Mick. I think it got to about number 21, really because it had Mick on it rather than any other reason. Mick called me over again a bit later and said he'd got another song, "Out Of Time". So Mick played a very rough version of it to me and I thought it was OK. When we got in to the studio, the riff at the beginning with the cellos was really catchy, but I still didn't think it would do anything because I had made so many singles before. I remember everyone sat around and said "This is it". I just thought I'd better forget about it . . . and then it was number 1 about a month after that.'

Chris Farlowe's version of 'Out Of Time', produced by Mick, was still riding high in the charts as the Stones were completing their fifth extensive American tour. They had become as popular in the States as they were in Britain. 'They took black American music and rechannelled it through their own whiteness,' explained Judy Sims. 'They made it much more palatable to the great masses of the American public because even though black music is certainly more acceptable than it used to be, most American music listeners and buyers can still relate to the white translation more than the black original. But the Rolling Stones don't just rechannel it; they make it as exciting or even more exciting through their own stage presence and through Mick's incredible personality. The only thing I can compare it to – and I'm not even sure if it's a good comparison – is Jimi Hendrix, because Hendrix also captured that sexual fantasy imagination. It has to do with clothes and movement and a kind of, not really sadistic, but the dark side of the personality. You wonder what it is really like, what he would do to me because he's so outrageous on stage, surely he must be outrageous alone in a dark room. It's that fantasy. It's something in the female psyche that is attracted to a man who might not be kind, considerate or necessarily affectionate.'

Meanwhile, the Stones were planning their very first Greatest Hits compilation titled *Big Hits (High Tide And Green Grass)*. The job of organising photo sessions for the cover was left to Andrew. He contacted various photographers to work on shots of the band in order to compile a colour booklet that would accompany the album and make up the bulk of the record's packaging. It would show the band captured in Olympic Studios, looking pale, weary and fatigued. Their clothes were just like any other high-street clothes; anyone could have them, but theirs were the extreme of it.

And to follow this, an announcement was made by Allen Klein that the Stones were expected to gross in excess of £20 million in the coming year. The figure, he said, would be made up chiefly from record royalties, tours and box office takings from two proposed films that he had planned for the band.

He had also planned for the Stones to appear on their old favourite, *The Ed Sullivan Show*, to push the new single 'Let's Spend The Night Together'. Wary of the song's lyrics, the show's producers insisted that the Stones compromise and change the chorus line to 'Let's spend some time together'.

'Even the Stones compromise sometimes,' reflected Bill. But they did not compromise on the massively popular *Sunday Night At The London Palladium* when they refused to mount the revolving carousel with all the other performers at the end of the show. Outraged headlines followed, but the Stones' view was 'All press is good press', particularly when it is two days after the release of their sixth album *Between The Buttons*. It was their last album as pop stars before entering the mythic phase. It was also their last album with Andrew producing. He always wanted the Stones to make the kind of records he wanted to listen to himself; songs about bitchy models, bored housewives and derailed heiresses . . .

By now Mick had been seen in public with Marianne Faithfull, although he was still living with his girlfriend Chrissie Shrimpton at Harley House in Marylebone Street, London. Marianne first met Jagger at Adrienne Posta's launch party in March 1964, but at that time she 'didn't care a damn about Mick or the Rolling Stones. I wouldn't even have known he was there if he hadn't had a flaming row with Chrissie. She was crying and shouting at him, and in the heat of the argument her false eyelashes were peeling off.'

Marianne's first record, 'As Tears Go By', had been written by Mick and Keith, and became a huge international hit. She had talent, charm, intelligence and beauty, and she was now beginning to settle into a love affair with Mick Jagger. Her life would soon look like a rock 'n' roll fairy tale. 'I thought it was a very glamorous period,' recalls Tony King. 'I think it's where the women became, for a while, almost as important as the group themselves. Marianne was very much a star in her own right, and I think she was responsible for giving Mick the more cultural image that he acquired at the time, and Anita was this very exotic international girl who would get on a plane with a rucksack on her back and a credit card in her pocket. They were absolutely the right girls for the right guys.'

Marianne had already been to a Stones recording session with Mick and found that she could easily be very bored. 'Stones sessions were less tiresome than most because they were almost always social events with lots of people hanging out in the studio. I remember they were finishing *Between The Buttons* at the end of 1966. They had been on tour constantly throughout the year and had spent little time in the studio. The sessions seemed to go on for ages. Most of their energy went into "Ruby Tuesday" and "Let's Spend The Night Together", the two love songs from the album which both became hit singles. For ages "Ruby Tuesday" had no lyrics, just this beautiful melody. It was very simple and that's how Brian loved it most. Brian's recorder dominates that song, it's a second vocal, a plaintive gull hovering over the song. It was really Brian's and Keith's song. Mick, who'd collaborated with Keith on all the Stones' originals for the last four years, had little to do with "Ruby Tuesday". He just came in to put on the vocals. Brian knew that it was one of the best things that he'd ever done and wanted everyone to say "That's great Brian, wonderful, good work", but of course nobody ever did. When the tension became unbearable, Mick and I would go up to the top of Olympic, where there were lots of empty rooms piled with old papers and crates, and we would smoke a joint and make love.'

Meanwhile, Les Perrin, a former Fleet Street journalist and publicity man, had been hired as the Stones' official publicist. Brian had been infuriated at the way the interviews following the Palladium incident had only featured Mick, and through Perrin arranged a series of interviews for himself. These interview requests were closely vetted by both Andrew and Klein, who only gave the go-ahead for Brian to talk to the music papers. But they had not bargained for the article in *News Of The World* which read 'Jagger told us I don't go much on it [LSD]; now the fans have taken it up, it'll just get a dirty name. I remember the first time I took it, I was on tour with Bo Diddley and Little Richard. During the time we were at Blazes club in Kensington, London, Jagger took about six Benzedrine tablets. I just wouldn't keep awake in places like this if I didn't have them. Later at Blazes, Jagger showed a companion and two girls a small piece of hash (marijuana) and invited them to his flat for a smoke.'

It became obvious, very quickly, that Mick had been mistaken for Brian. The whole affair, it was feared, was set to have far greater repercussions than a simple cockeyed *News Of The World* exposé.

'The police went round searching everyone and taking pieces of evidence, doggedly collecting incense and miniature bars of hotel soap in their flat-footed way. Then they came for the green velvet jacket with the four pills of speed in it. When they asked who the pills belonged to, Mick very gallantly said they were his. The worst thing that happened was that they found heroin on Robert.'

Keith made plans to escape the frenzied media attention and Brian suggested that he and Anita should join him. They set off in Keith's Bentley, crossing the Channel to France without incident until they got to the Spanish border, where Brian overdosed in the back of the car and was rushed to a Spanish hospital for emergency treatment and was kept there for several days. 'So there's me and Anita,' explains Keith, 'and amazing things can happen in the back of a car, and they did. He caught up with us back in London, where there was this tearful scene.' In reality, the trip turned out to be the elopement of Keith and Anita. 'He never forgave me for that,' continues Keith, 'and I don't blame him, but it happens.'

Charges were eventually brought against Mick, Keith and Robert, who on 10 May appeared at Chichester Crown Court in Sussex, where they elected to be tried by jury. All three were bound over on £100 bail and ordered to appear again at the West Sussex Quarter sessions on 27 June. 'Crowds of people were excluded from the court hearing because of lack of space,' reported the BBC News team. 'The forty-two public seats were taken by young fans, many of whom had hitch-hiked overnight from London so they could be first in the queue. Teenagers, of course, weren't the only ones who wanted to see the pop stars Mick Jagger and Keith Richard . . . many of them were parents who came with tiny tots. One woman even wanted to take her pet into court. The two Rolling Stones were smuggled into court the back way having left Richard's home at West Wittering about 8 miles away, and having swapped cars on route.'

The weeks between trials were, unsurprisingly, non-productive, feeding Andrew's anxieties that the end of the Stones looked a real possibility. They were due to start work on a follow-up studio album to the Big Hits collection, but instead, Mick, Keith and Marianne went to the EMI studios in Abbey Road in order to attend the BBC's live broadcast for the *Our World* programme. This was an ambitious attempt to bring the populations of five continents together through music. The show was watched by an estimated audience of 400 million people. The Britlish offering was a performance by the Beatles with their message for the world 'All You Need Is Love'.

Two days later, on 27 June, the Jagger/Richard/Fraser trial started at the West Sussex Quarter Sessions, concluding on the 29 June. During this time the normally sleepy town of Chichester was turned into a circus, with hotdog and ice cream stalls, balloon sellers and a fun fair creating a party-like atmosphere normally reserved for state visits.

'All the teenage screaming and blustering vanished at the moment Judge Block passed sentence,' reported Clifford Luton for BBC News. 'As he said sternly to Richard that the offence to which he had been found guilty carried a maximum sentence of ten years, there was a gasp of horror from the youngsters crowded in the public gallery, but there was a dead silence as the judge added "You will go to prison for one year and you will pay £500 towards the cost of the prosecution. Go down." Richard, who earlier had talked in his evidence of what he called petty morals, went down to the cells without expression. Robert Hugh Fraser, sentenced to six months and £200 costs, also walked away with an expressionless face. Jagger, who was wearing a primrose frilled shirt with pleated yellow lace cuffs, put his hand to his face as he was given three months with £100 costs. For a moment, he looked like fainting and then prison officers moved forward to take his arms and help him down to the cells.'

Jagger, Richard and Fraser were hustled into a police van and driven to London, where their first stop was Brixton Prison, where Mick would be staying for the next three months, while Keith and Robert Fraser were bound for Wormwood Scrubs.

As soon as the sentencing was completed an appeal was granted with a preliminary hearing set for the next day, when Mick and Keith were released on bail of £7,000 each. Robert did not fare so well, his application was turned down.

For once, some of the newspapers were saying how harshly the two Rolling Stones had been treated, and on 1 July *The Times* carried a long editorial attacking the manner in which the case had been conducted and suggesting that in Mick's case particularly justice had not necessarily been seen to be done. 'Mr Jagger has been sentenced to imprisonment for three months,' wrote William Rees-Mogg, editor of *The Times*. 'He is appealing against conviction and sentence, and has been granted bail until the hearing of the appeal later in the year. In the meantime, the sentence of imprisonment is bound to be widely discussed by the public. And the circumstances are sufficiently unusual to warrant such discussion in the public interest.

'Mr Jagger was charged with being in possession of four tablets containing amphetamine sulphate and methyl amphetamine hydrochloride; these tablets had been bought perfectly legally in Italy and brought back to this country. They are not a highly dangerous drug or, in proper dosage, a dangerous drug at all. They are of the Benzedrine type and the Italian manufacturers recommend them both as a stimulant and as a remedy for travel sickness.

'In Britain, it is an offence to possess these drugs without a doctor's prescription. Mr Jagger's doctor says that he knew and had authorised their use, but he did not give a prescription for them as indeed they had already been purchased. His evidence was not challenged. This was, therefore, an offence of a technical character which before this case drew the point to public attention any honest man might have been liable to commit. If, after his visit to the Pope, the Archbishop of Canterbury had bought proprietary air sickness pills at Rome Airport and imported the unused tablets into Britain on his return, he would have risked committing precisely the same offence. No-one who has ever travelled and bought proprietary drugs abroad can be sure that he has not broken the law.

'Judge Block directed the jury that the approval of a doctor is not a defence in law to the charge of possessing drugs without a prescription, and the jury convicted. Mr Jagger was not charged with complicity in any other drug offence that occurred in the same house. They were separate cases, and no evidence was produced to suggest that he knew Mr Fraser had heroin tablets or that the vanishing Mr Sniderman had cannabis resin. It is indeed no offence to be in the same building, or the same company as people possessing, or even using drugs, nor could it reasonably be made an offence. The drugs which Mr Jagger had in his possession must therefore be treated on their own as a separate issue from the other drugs that other people may have had in their possession at the same time. It may be difficult for lay opinion to make this distinction clearly, but obviously justice cannot be done if one man is to be punished for a purely contingent association with someone else's offence.

Photo by Pictorial Press Ltd

Mick with Marianne Faithfull, arrested during a police raid • Photo by Range Pictures Ltd

'We have, therefore, a conviction against Mr Jagger purely on the grounds that he possessed four Italian pep pills, quite legally bought, but not legally imported without a prescription. Four is not a large number. This is not the quantity which a pusher of drugs would have on him, nor even the quantity one would expect in an addict. In any case, Mr Jagger's career is obviously one that does involve great personal strain and exhaustion; his doctor says that he approved the occasional use of these drugs, and it seems likely that similar drugs would have been prescribed if there was a need for them. Millions of similar drugs would have been prescribed in Britain every year, and for a variety of conditions. One has to ask, therefore, how it is that this technical offence, divorced as it must be from other people's offences, was thought to deserve the penalty of imprisonment. In the courts at large it is most uncommon for imprisonment to be imposed on first offenders where the drugs are not major drugs of addiction and there is no question of drug traffic. The normal penalty is probation, and the purpose of probation is to encourage the offender to develop his career and to avoid the drug risks in future. It is surprising, therefore, that Judge Block should have decided to sentence Mr Jagger to imprisonment and particularly surprising as Mr Jagger's is about as mild a drug case as can ever have been brought before the courts.

'It would be wrong to speculate on the judge's reasons, which we do not know. It is, however, possible to consider the public reaction. There are many people who take a primitive view of the matter, what one might call a pre-legal view of the matter. They consider that Mr Jagger has "got what was coming to him". They resent the anarchic quality of the Rolling Stones' performances, dislike their songs, dislike their influence on teenagers and broadly suspect them of decadence, a word used by Miss Monica Fulong in the *Daily Mail*.

Mick and Keith after attending court in Chichester, 1967 • Photo by Popperfoto

'As a sociological concern, this may be reasonable enough, and at an emotional level it is very understandable, but it has nothing at all to do with the case. One has to ask a different question: has Mr Jagger received the same treatment as he would have received if he had not been a famous figure, with all the criticism his celebrity has aroused? If a promising undergraduate had come back from a summer visit to Italy with four pep pills in his pocket, would it have been thought necessary to display him, handcuffed, to the public? There are cases in which a single figure becomes the focus for public concern about some aspects of public morality. The Stephen Ward case, with its dubious evidence and questionable verdict was one of them, and that verdict killed Stephen Ward. There are elements of the same emotions in the reactions to this case. If we are going to make any case a symbol of the conflict between the sound traditional values of Britain and the new hedonism, then we must be sure that the sound traditional values include those of tolerance and equity. It should be the particular quality of British justice to ensure that Mr Jagger is treated exactly the same as anyone else, no better and no worse. There must remain a suspicion in this case that Mr Jagger received a more severe sentence than would have been thought proper for any purely anonymous young man.'

History has not recorded how Brian felt about the public downfall of Jagger and Richard. He was probably too concerned about facing his own trial on a drugs charge from June, which had now been set for 30 October at the Inner London Sessions.

In the meantime, on 31 July, the Appeals Court lifted the sentences. Keith's conviction was squashed, and Mick was given a conditional discharge. 'It was a painful year,' Keith remembers. 'It was a big year of change for everybody. 1967 was the explosion of the drug culture, if there is such a thing. That's when it came into the open from underground. Everybody started talking about it. And throughout this whole year, we were having to put up with this incredible hassle, this confrontation with policeman and judges. I feel very uncomfortable looking at a uniform anyway, and having to deal with these people for a whole year did wear us down a bit. In fact, it put us on our back really for eighteen months or so. It wasn't until we got into *Beggars' Banquet* that the whole thing managed to slide into the past. Though at the time it was still bugging Brian like mad . . . and Mick. I suppose it was the fact that so many people, including the press, or sections of it, had been dying for so long to have a go at us. There are certain things which went on behind the scenes which are very unsavoury, and which once and for all destroyed my faith in the fairness and impartiality of the British judicial system. Only when you create a fuss and get it up to the highest level do they start to reconsider. When the prosecuting council asked me about chicks in nothing but fur rugs, I said I'm not concerned with your petty morals, which are illegitimate. They couldn't take that one. When it came down to it, they couldn't pin anything at all on us. All they could pin on me was allowing people to smoke on my premises. It wasn't my shit. All they could pin on Mick were these four amphetamine tablets he'd bought in Italy over the counter. It really backfired on them because they didn't get enough on us. They had more on the people who were with us who they weren't interested in.'

Without recording commitments for the Stones, Brian paid a visit to Olympic Studios and sat in with the Beatles. They had taken to recording there, and Brian sang backing vocals on 'Baby, You're A Rich Man'. A few weeks later he took up another invitation to sit in with them on a session at a studio in London's Kingsway. It was the third time he had been asked to contribute something to a Beatles recording. The first time he had provided the hand claps on 'Yellow Submarine'. This time he contributed some guitar work to 'You Know My Name, Look Up My Number', and according to Paul McCartney had played in exactly the style they wanted.

Photo by Pictorial Press Ltd

The band's next move was to sort out their management. Oldham had long since distanced himself from the band's activities and, not surprisingly, had experienced a shift of attitude from them because of it. The group's displeasure mainly stemmed from Oldham's snubbing of the band when things got tough.

Andrew had lost his grip over the band. It couldn't have been any clearer that they had outgrown him. The final split came at a session at the Olympic Studios. 'There was definitely a feeling from the Rolling Stones that I had let them down morally during the drugs trial,' remarks Andrew. 'I cannot defend myself on that factor except to say that I thought it vitally important in the continuation of business for all of us that one of us was not busted, so I was making sure I wasn't, to carry out their business in any territory of the world. For example, if some publisher in Australia had been screwing us, I could go down there and get the bread. I didn't want a situation where I would arrive at Sydney Airport and be turned back by immigration. I was applying logic to the situation . . . and to be quite honest, if I had continued at the speed they were continuing at, I would not be alive today.'

In September, the Stones flew to New York to meet with Klein and to inform him of Oldham's departure. It was agreed that Klein would assume all responsibilities for management and production, but the job of finding a new producer fell to Mick. He contacted a guy called Jimmy Miller, who had previously worked with Traffic and the Spencer Davis Group:

'I came home one night and my wife said Mick Jagger called and wants you to call him back . . . he's left his number. I just got a flash as she said that, that he wants me to produce them, so I very nervously called up, and Mick said "Jimmy can you come by? I'd like to talk to you about something". I stopped by his house, had some tea, and sat and talked for a few minutes. He said he'd been aware of my productions for some time, and told me that they were splitting up or had split up with Andrew. Then he said they were looking for a producer and asked if I'd be interested. It was as simple as that! They had material at that time for an album which was to become *Beggars' Banquet*, which was the first series of sessions that we worked on. I think the first track we cut was "Street Fighting Man", but the first one we finished was "Jumping Jack Flash", which was issued as a single prior to the album, so that was my first release as a producer with the Stones.'

By now, Brian had appeared at the Inner London Sessions and had been found guilty of possession of cannabis, the drugs charge from June. He was sentenced to prison terms of nine months and three months to run concurrently. He was also ordered to pay 10 and 50 guineas in costs. Pandemonium broke out in the public gallery. Brian was taken to Wormwood Scrubs to begin his sentence, although the next day he was released on £750 bail pending an appeal. Within two months, on 12 December, Brian's appeal was heard in the Court of Criminal Appeal in Fleet Street where his nine month sentence was set aside in favour of a £1,000 fine and a three-year probation. On the same day, the Stones released their seventh and long-awaited album, *Their Satanic Majesties' Request*. Brian had predicted that this album would be greeted as a commercial and critical failure – which of course it was. The one thing that characterised this period was the way things were packaged and presented. Album jacket design in particular became as important as the product itself: colourful, bright, bold, loud and most of all exciting. With their new album the Rolling Stones embodied this awareness, but in truth, their latest release was no more than a second-rate 'Sergeant Pepper' and, in Brian's mind, commercial rubbish. He considered the band's departure from the blues as a colossal error.

Photo by Pictorial Press Ltd

Brian clearly saw that the Stones needed to pull themselves together musically, and he seized the opportunity to lead the way in the studio. Brian envisaged shaping and evolving heavier and rockier riffs in a bid to return their sound to its pre-psychedelic and pop glory. It was something that they all realised was essential, yet Brian now seemed totally uninterested in his career as a Rolling Stone. He was only in the studio on rare occasions, one time to record his guitar part for 'Jumping Jack Flash' and at other times for the latter stages of the recording of the *Beggars' Banquet* album.

'When I first became associated with the Stones,' remembers Jimmy Miller, 'it was after the point when Brian had started to leave – his exit was a very slow one. It was due to an increasing difference in musical direction and various other problems. Though Brian appears on *Beggars' Banquet*, playing flute on one track, percussion on another and sitar on another, there was perhaps a lack of interest on Brian's part – out of frustration maybe – and so his appearances at the sessions were less and less frequent. It required a lot from Keith because Brian hadn't left officially, so they couldn't get someone else in, yet Brian couldn't be counted on to be there.'

While Brian's contribution to the Stones continued to be on a level of non-participation, he did hold on long enough to join the band on a surprise, and by now rare, appearance playing live at the *New Musical Express* Poll Winners concert at the Empire Pool, Wembley, where they would receive the award for best R&B band. It was the group's first public appearance in Britain for nearly two years, but it was to be Brian's last.

'Rock 'n' Roll Circus' filmed live at Wembley studios, December 1968 • Photo by Rex Features

CHAPTER 6

A Rock 'n' Roll Circus

The Rolling Stones Rock and Roll Circus was the title of the band's planned colour television spectacular for world distribution in December 1968. The group had hired a big top from Sir Robert Fossett's circus, complete with jugglers, acrobats, clowns and wild animals, in order to stage an event featuring the cream of British rock talent. The line-up included the Who, Eric Clapton, Jethro Tull, John Lennon and, of course, the Rolling Stones.

Brian, still uninterested in his career as a Rolling Stone, lamely strummed along with the band on half a dozen new numbers from their forthcoming album *Beggars' Banquet*, with the same level of non-participation as before. It would be his last appearance with the band, and one that has never been seen, as Jagger considered the whole performance below par and consequently shelved the film. He did, however, have other ideas for it. 'I had an idea of doing a fantasy movie on the Rolling Stones of which that would be part . . . a really long one, like two hours long, with some old songs that have never been heard, and new ones. I just never brought it to fruition because of other things. The people on television are very choosy about what they want to see, you'd be surprised. They'd probably cut it up and spend a lot of time, and send it to one of the English TV companies, and turn it down because you can't get the money back from the BBC because they just don't have the budgets.'

Meanwhile, 'Street Fighting Man' was released as the new single. It was met with disapproval by the radio stations in America, who refused to play it on the grounds that it could incite further riots on the streets of Los Angeles. Back in England, the release date of the *Beggars' Banquet* album had been put back due to a censorship problem with the cover. It was just a photo of a toilet with graffiti, cleverly intermixed with the credits and everything. This original cover was rejected by the label, and in the end Mick just told them to find the most 'proper' artist with regard to text and have them lay out the cover as tastefully as possible on an off-white background.

By the time *Beggars' Banquet* was out, the Stones were facing a crippling tax demand. They desperately needed to tour again, but Brian was not physically or mentally capable of sustaining a tour. It was obvious that there was never going to be a better or easier time to rid themselves of their one-time leader. For his major contribution to the music of the Stones, and for his formation of the band, Mick and Keith would offer Brian a conscience-easing £100,000 as an initial payment for leaving the group plus £20,000 per year as long as the Stones stayed together as a band.

Although Allen Klein was not pleased with the settlement being proposed, he agreed to it because as far as he was concerned the sooner Jones was out of the band the better. Without further delay Mick, Keith and Charlie broke the news to Brian that they were kicking him out of the band, and to all intents and purposes had already replaced him with former John Mayall guitarist Mick Taylor. 'It was me that got Mick Taylor into this,' claims Ian. 'There weren't really very many choices, only really him and Ronnie Wood, but after a really lean time the Faces were just starting to look up again with Ronnie playing with them, so Ronnie Laine said, "For Christ's sake don't pinch him, we need him." When I thought about Mick Taylor, Jagger didn't even realise who he was. He was thinking about somebody else. It was really on John Mayall's recommendation because, as I see it, anybody who John Mayall can put up with has got to be good, and also has to be a fairly easy-going guy to put up with John Mayall. So he seemed like the obvious person.'

The announcement that Brian Jones had left the Stones, possibly to rejoin them at some later date, was made in May 1969. Simultaneously it was announced that 21-year-old Mick Taylor would be joining. Taylor was born on 17 January 1948 in Welwyn Garden City, Hertfordshire. His father, Lionel, was an aircraft worker. He went to Onslow Secondary Modern School but left at fifteen and worked as a commercial artist for three months, then as a labourer in a paint factory. Taylor taught himself to play guitar and joined a local band called the Gods. When Eric Clapton missed a gig with John Mayall's Bluesbreakers, Mick deputised for him and later, when Clapton left, Taylor was called in as his replacement. Now he was being called in to replace Brian Jones, the founder of the Rolling Stones.

'The first time I ever heard him or saw him was around '66, when Jack Bruce and Eric Clapton were in the band, and Eric didn't show up for a gig one night,' reminisces John Mayall. 'This was in Welwyn Garden City at some community hall. So we played it as a trio without a guitarist. This kid came up and said that he'd been to the Flamingo a lot, and knew all the numbers that we were likely to play. He said he'd listened to Eric a lot and he asked if he could play with us. So, thinking we had nothing to lose, we let him have a go. He came on for the second set, and played really quite acceptably, almost note for note copying Clapton at that time. I ran into him again about a year later, when he was playing in a group called the Gods, and they were doing "Hideaway" and a lot of other stuff revolving round Freddie King. Then when Eric left, we had the Peter Green phase, which was another year, and after Fleetwood Mac was spawned it left me with another band to form. I put an advert for a guitarist in the *Melody Maker*, and got thoroughly frightened because the first morning after the paper came out, there were about a hundred guys ringing up and it just got mind-boggling. By then, I was desperate for somebody that I vaguely knew, so when Mick rang up and identified himself as the person who had sat in that time I gave him the job straight away. That was the summer of 1967.

'A couple of years later, Mick Jagger got in touch with me, and I went to see him at the recording studio. He was recording "You Can't Always Get What You Want" with the mass London English Choir, or whatever it was, and we talked about Mick Taylor then. Apparently, he called Mick up the next day, and it was all very convenient as regards timing.'

Brian also made an announcement, saying: 'I no longer see eye to eye with the others over the discs we are cutting. We no longer communicate musically. The Stones' music is not to my taste any more. The work of Mick and Keith has progressed at a tangent, at least to my way of thinking. I have a desire to play my own brand of music rather than that of others no matter how I appreciate their musical concepts.

'We had a friendly meeting and agreed that an amicable termination, temporary or permanent, was the only answer. The only solution was to go our separate ways, but we shall remain friends.' The press relayed the story with an undertone of "Did he jump, or was he pushed?", and the fans met the news with a certain resignation.

Brian's path from the Stones had led him to the door of author A.A. Milne's hideaway, Cotchford Farm, on the outskirts of the Ashdown Forest in Sussex – the scene of Brian's final weeks alive. Now no longer a Rolling Stone, Brian set about rebuilding his life and was, as many people said, full of hope for the future. His plans for a new group were reaching fruition, and he had even visited the Stones at Olympic Studios, where they were cutting some tracks for the *Let It Bleed* album with new Stone, Mick Taylor. They were also preparing themselves, and Taylor, for the concert at Hyde Park in London.

'We had about three weeks to set it up from the time that they decided they would do Hyde Park,' recalls Jo Bergman, the Stones' right-hand lady at that time. 'We were working with Andrew King and Sam Butler at Blackhill Enterprises and the park department, who were very concerned because they thought the Rolling Stones would do incredible damage to their lovely park. So Mick went down to see one of the officials who looks after parks and said "We don't want to kill the flowers and the trees either".

'New Stone' Mick Taylor is introduced to the press in Hyde Park • Photo by Popperfoto

'Of course, they wouldn't let us advertise, so Mick got very worried because he thought nobody would turn up. He was starting to do a lot of interviews and one or two radio bits, and he'd just say "See you in the Park on Saturday." We kept saying to Mick "Look, people will come, there will be thousands there", and of course there were. It was a lovely day, but of course it was just after Brian's death, and no-one was expecting that.'

The Stones had heard the news of Brian's death while they were recording at Olympic on the evening of 3 July. The session was booked to start around midnight, but it was not until about ten past one that Ian received the call. Everyone there was stunned and dazed. 'It was a terrible shock,' remembers Keith. 'I always knew Brian was a very fragile person. When I think about it, there are certain people you meet, and Brian was probably one of them, who you couldn't imagine getting old. He's one of those people who you know are going to go fairly young, because they burn it all up so quick. Nevertheless, that didn't lessen the shock when it happened. Being with that cat for seven or eight years non-stop, you know, to have him suddenly removed completely. It really knocked us back.'

The tributes to Brian appeared on the front pages of all the daily newspapers that same morning with the news that Brian had been found dead in his swimming pool. Obviously enough, the Stones' Hyde Park concert in London only two days later became a tribute to the memory of Brian. Mick asked the audience for silence as he read two verses from Shelley's 'Adonais', before releasing hundreds of butterflies.

To some extent, the logistics of the concert staging were dictated by the fact that it was being filmed by Granada Television. The pressure of organisation fell to Andrew King, who worked for the promoters Blackhill Enterprises. 'There were about 250,000 people wanting press tickets from all round the world, so there were certain problems which we could anticipate with the number of people wanting to be in the stage area. Of course, when it started happening it was absolutely chronic. It was so crowded inside that to move from the dressing room caravans to the stage it was necessary to have about ten huge people heaving at the crowd just to move through, just to get to the stage. I couldn't believe how awful it was around the stage, and then Marianne arrives, and all the other ladies arrive, and their young children, and there are others with vaguely familiar faces. They all start turning up in limos and where are you going to put them all, there's just nowhere to put them. I remember at one point, I tried to get people off the stage and I went up to Allen Klein and said "Would you get off the stage please?" I knew who he was. He said "Listen, you get all those people out there off the stage, and then you come back and ask me to get off the stage." It was amazing, but then it felt so incredibly crowded that the whole thing was just going to collapse under the pressure. I remember climbing up on to one of the PA towers, and from there I could see what was going on around: in every direction I looked, as far as I could see, quarter of a mile in any direction, it was just solid people, absolutely solid.'

On top of that, there were other problems that weren't anticipated. 'What was meant to happen,' continues Andrew, 'was that Sam Culver was supposed to have got together about forty stewards from the people who did the steward things at the Roundhouse and whatever. We were getting them through various organisations, and they were all meant to be down there to be briefed on the evening before, but Sam never got it together. He was quite a terror at that sort of thing. So when we went down there early in the morning, we found about 15,000 people who had slept in the park, and by 6.30 a.m. a big crowd was already round the stage. We had no stewards, so at the time it was a question of doing the best with the resources we had. There were all these Hell's Angels, so

Shopgirls Jennie Hyde and Penny Smith at the funeral of Brian Jones, July 1969 • Photo by Popperfoto

Brian had been one of the highest-paid musicians and performers in pop music, yet at the time of his death the ex-Rolling Stone was broke. His promised pay-off settlement of £100,000 from the band, had never materialised, nor had any of his retainer totalling £20,000 per annum. As early as 1968, Brian's affairs were wildly out of hand, and he was deeply in debt. The true extent of these debts was disclosed at a creditors' meeting a year after his death. Yet Brian was no spendthrift. He had his Rolls Royce and his clothes but he did not waste money. He was milked dry by a few hangers-on, despite being a very intelligent individual. Brian was never the richest member of the Stones: Mick Jagger and Keith Richards received the lion's share of the royalties as they were the band's song-writers.

Undoubtedly things had changed for the Stones. Mick had distanced himself from the band, if only for a short time, to focus on his acting, while the others added their finishing touches to the tracks already laid down for the *Let It Bleed* album. But individually they were feeling strong and decisive about going back on the road for the first time in three years.

Plans quickly got underway for a North American tour of arenas to kick off that November in support of the album's release. 'It had changed while we'd been off the road,' observed Keith. 'We suddenly got to work with PA systems, and there was an audience who were listening instead of screaming chicks. Instead of playing full blast just to try and penetrate the audience, suddenly it was back to learning how to play on stage again. So for us, the '69 tour was like a school again.'

Jo Bergman brought in Chip Monck, one of the people responsible for putting on Woodstock, to come up with something new in the way of lighting and staging. 'I called Mick in Mount Ferry in New South Wales while he was doing *Ned Kelly*, and tried to explain what I would do,' recalls Chip. 'Then I went ahead and built it, or got it together as much as I could, and met up with them when I came into Los Angeles just before the tour. We had such triumphs, like the eight o'clock first show at the Los Angeles Forum went up at 11.30 and the second show began at 2.45 in the morning! I didn't have any help until I hired Bill Beaumont of Country Joe and the Fish fame to assist me in getting pieces of equipment from A to B, and personnel, and the group, but this was disastrous . . . I saw no reason whatsoever why they would have wanted to continue with me!'

In fact, the Stones did continue working with Chip, and eventually the tour was very successful. They had Ike and Tina Turner opening the shows, whipping the crowds up in readiness for the Stones' set, which drove them into pure ecstasy. It became one of the most fondly remembered tours in rock 'n' roll history, until one gig went horribly wrong, and would dog their career for years to come.

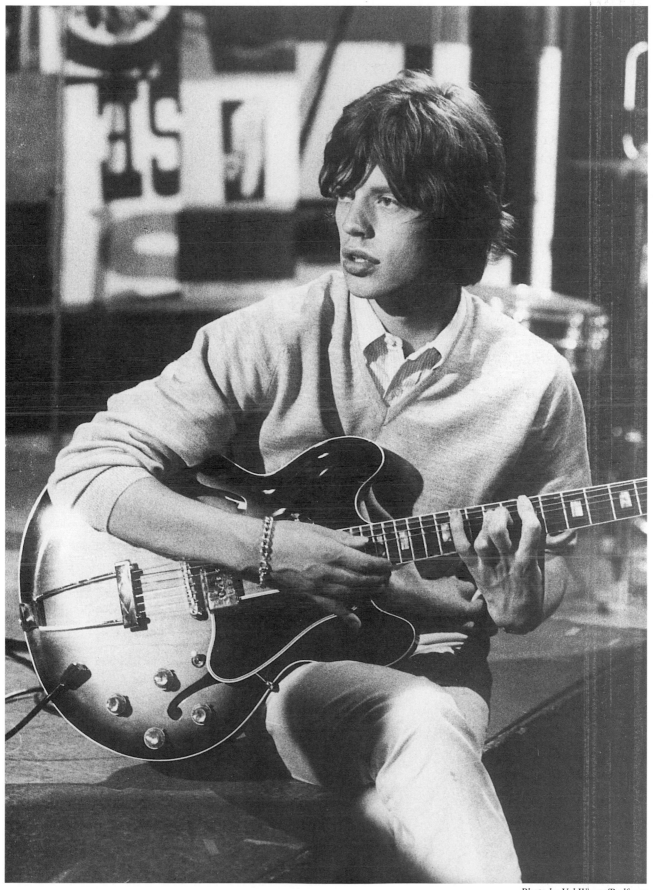

Photo by Val Wimer/Redferns

Keith in his Cheyne Walk flat with the silver disc for 'Honky Tonk Women', 1969 • Photo by Barry Plummer

CHAPTER 7

Everybody Seems To Be Ready. Are You Ready?

From the specially rigged stage at the Altamont Speedway, near Livermore in northern California, Mick addressed an uneasy crowd: 'Just be cool down the front here, and don't push around. Everyone sit down and just keep cool. Let's just relax, let's just get into a groove, we can get it together.' But sadly no-one did, least of all the Stones.

The morning of 6 December had started a very beautiful laid-back Californian day. 'I remember walking through a very relaxed crowd,' remarked Charlie. 'There was the "love and peace" bit as well, but then it all got very nasty. I remember walking on stage and heard these guys grunting like "Get out the way", and from then on, the whole crowd went like that, and I knew something wasn't quite right.'

The Stones were giving a free concert as a thank-you to the fans for their loyalty and support through the years, but the idea would bear tragic results. To bring in the Hell's Angels to help police the crowds and act as security, as they had with the Hyde Park concert, was probably the most serious oversight. The difference was that these were American Hell's Angels, and unlike those in England, they would be inflamed by drugs and alcohol. As a result they laid into the crowd, hitting and beating the fans with their billiard cues as well as driving their motorcycles straight at them in what appeared a blatant attempt to maim and injure. The violence reached horrific proportions when a girl had her ankle broken as bikes were overturned on top of her, an 18-year-old coloured boy was surrounded by Hell's Angels and stabbed to death with their billiard cues, and in the crush dozens more were injured.

'There were other oversights,' recalls Chip Monck. 'When we were using the Filmways property at another raceway in the San Francisco area, the stage was going to be at the top of a hill, so it was

3ft 6in high and that was lovely. When we moved it to Altamont overnight, it went into a valley and as a result it was much too low. We lost a lot of equipment, I lost a lot of teeth, it was a horror show . . . and I have a feeling that the majority of blame can be shared by those who failed to organise the facility correctly, the security, the people. We all bear some blame, but most of us have taken it as a very good lesson. I certainly hope those people didn't die for nothing.'

The responsibility of organisation fell to Sam Cutler, who since his excellent job as compere at Hyde Park was working with the Stones on this tour. 'Within twenty-four hours we moved everything from the original site in Sinoma County to the Altamont site, which as a logistical exercise has never been equalled since. We moved tons of equipment, more equipment than I've ever seen any band get their hands on. We moved from here to there, and we did it all with volunteers. We were sitting in our office with cameras and lights, and we would just go on the radio or the television saying that we needed this or we needed that. It was just a very low point in the quality of the Rolling Stones set-up. It was bitterly cold, it was the wrong time of the year to do the concert, we were in the wrong place, the stage was the wrong height, the media gave it far too much prominence and blew the thing completely out of hand, so by the time the concert happened it all just turned into an awful anti-climax and the net result was that hundreds of people died. It was a disaster.'

'I thought the show would have been stopped,' remarks Keith, 'but hardly anyone seemed to want to take any notice. The violence in front of the stage was incredible. Looking back, I don't think it was a good idea to have the Hell's Angels, but the Grateful Dead – who've organised these shows before – thought they would be best. I believe the alternative would have been the Black Panthers. I wouldn't like to say whether they would have been more vicious.'

The Stones made a hurried departure from Altamont by helicopter, but the incident dogged their careers for many years after. 'The Altamont thing was really nasty,' recalls Mick, 'a very nasty experience, but it didn't completely sully the tour for me. That was one gig that went really wrong, and it was outside the experience of that tour, which was a tour of arenas. Yes, it was a complete mess and we were partly to blame for not checking it out. It was just totally disorganised. You'd expect everyone in San Francisco would be so mellow and nice and organised. We thought it was going to be all those things but of course it wasn't.'

By the time the Stones had returned to England following the ill-fated Altamont concert, Jean-Luc Godard's *One Plus One* had been released in the States, featuring the Stones recording 'Sympathy For The Devil'. To Godard's anger and distress, the film's producer, Ian Quarrier, changed the name of the film to the song title and a complete take of the song was edited into the film against Godard's wishes. In his review of the film on 27 April, the *New York Times* critic Roger Greenspun says: 'An English-language movie by Jean-Luc Godard opened theatrically yesterday at the Murray Hill. If you go on Monday, Wednesday, Friday or Sunday, you will see Godard's film, which is properly known as *One Plus One*. On other days, you will see a film popularly advertised as *Sympathy For The Devil*, which exactly resembles *One Plus One* except that in the latter part of the last reel a complete version of the song "Sympathy For The Devil", which the Rolling Stones have been rehearsing and recording in cuts throughout the film, is played on the soundtrack. Several monochromatic stills of the film's last shot are added to fill out the song's time.'

Meanwhile, whispers were circulating that all was not well between the Stones and Decca Records and there seemed to be some substance to them. Dick Rowe, for one, was beginning to feel undervalued. He felt that his role as A&R man was continually being undermined, particularly by Jagger.

Photo by Rex Features Ltd

'There are always problems arising as circumstances change,' observed Rowe. 'It's a bit like a marriage . . . it doesn't always stay quite like it is during the honeymoon. Although we had a great many differences, in the end Mick Jagger really didn't have much time for me personally, because my job does on occasions makes me have to act like a schoolmaster.'

In return, Jagger felt that Decca never co-operated with the band. As far as he was concerned, their strategies and suggestions for the group were no longer in tune with his own. The gap between them had now become a sufficient wedge for the Stones to look elsewhere for a record deal.

It left Decca without the 'jewel in their crown', but it also left the Stones owing the label one final track. Decca got their track, but the sexually explicit lyrics of 'Cocksucker Blues' made it unlikely that Decca would release it – and, sure enough, they didn't.

The great divide continued as the Stones filed a lawsuit against Allen Klein and ABKCO Industries Inc. claiming mishandling of Rolling Stones funds, saying that Klein persuaded the band to sign over all the North American rights of their songs to a company called Nanker Phelge Music Inc. The Stones claimed they were led to believe that they ran the company, when in truth it was controlled by Klein. This was followed by another High Court writ against ex-managers Andrew Oldham and Eric Easton, charging that they had made a secret deal with Decca Records in 1963 which deprived the group of record royalties. The suit alleged that Oldham persuaded Brian Jones to accept a 6 per cent share of wholesale record price as the Stones' share, while Decca was paying Oldham and Easton 14 per cent. At the same time, Oldham had a 25 per cent management contract with the Stones themselves. Both suits were signed by the four remaining original band members and Lewis Jones, Brian's father. Both cases were settled out of court in favour of the Stones.

Despite their reservations over Klein, Keith had no real regrets: 'He turned it into a global thing because he opened your eyes. Sure, he's gonna rip you off if he can, but loads of other cats are taking their piece anyway. I never learnt as much, and I never worried about who took what from who, here and there, so I figured it's the price of an education.' 'He did very good deals for us,' continues Bill, 'but I think he was really looking after himself first, and in retrospect that was the case.'

Strangely enough, Marianne had only met Klein a couple of times but immediately took a liking to him, so much so that she trusted him implicitly. She had quietly confided to him that she was actually in love with Keith. 'He made the situation simple by saying "But Marianne, if you go with Keith it will destroy Mick." And, of course, he was right, it would have been devastating, but it was also true all the time I was with Mick, I was in love with Mick.'

By now *Gimme Shelter*, the documentary film of the ill-fated 1969 US tour including footage of the Altamont concert shot by Albert and David Maysles, is premiered at the Plaza Theater in New York City. Within weeks the film clip that highlights the horrors of Altamont is run time and time again during the trial that found Hell's Angel Alan Passaro 'not guilty' in the death of 18-year-old Meredith Hunter, who had been brutally stabbed to death at the concert.

In the meantime, Marshall Chess had renewed his affiliation with the Stones. He was no longer with the Chess label in Chicago, and took the opportunity presented by a London visit to suggest to Jagger that the Stones launch their own label. 'It was really just a licensing deal,' recalls Mick. 'We didn't have a label with a host of other artists on it, but at least it gave us the image that we were independent.'

Meanwhile, the job of organising the sleeve design for their first album on their own label was left to Andy Warhol. The 'Sticky Fingers' cover incorporated a real zip on a pair of jeans. It involved months of work to discover a way to manufacture and package without causing damage to the records. 'We packed up boxes and mailed them to ourselves,' recalls Marshall Chess, 'just to see how they would ship. The first batch all had marks from the zipper on it, so we figured out that we should ship them with the zipper undone. That way, if there was pressure it would be in the middle of the label and not on the groove . . . lots of things like that. It finally came out on time. We made it right at the last minute, but up until the week before, we almost had to scrap that cover, we just couldn't figure out how to package it without damaging the records.'

Mick with Marianne Faithfull at the 'Blind Faith' concert, Hyde Park, 1969 • Photo by Retna Pictures

Keith with his wife, actress Anita Pallenberg, and their two children • Photo by Range Pictures Ltd

CHAPTER 8

Where To Now?

With no immediate recording or touring obligations, the Stones were now feeling a serious economic pinch which resulted in them becoming Britain's first rock 'n' roll tax exiles. 'The reason we left England and became tax exiles,' explains Mick, 'was because we were totally broke, and we owed the Inland Revenue more money than we could possibly earn when income tax was about 90 per cent or whatever it was. It was a pity we had to leave; it would not have been my choice.'

Mick moved into a house in Biot, Charlie found a farmhouse in the Cevennes, Mick Taylor went to live in Grasse, and Keith rented Nellcot, a huge villa on the coast at Villefranche-sur-Mer, where the Stones Mobile was stationed. This was a large khaki camouflaged trailer truck that housed £100,000 worth of sixteen-track equipment to convert Keith's basement into a studio.

'When we left England and went to France,' continues Bill, 'we had no money. On a million dollars, you got left with 70,000 and you owed more than that to the tax people. We couldn't win; we had to leave. But then you become bad boys again – you get accused of becoming tax exiles to line your pockets.'

Reports in the *Daily Telegraph* suggested that the fortune of the Rolling Stones from recordings alone was estimated in the region of £83 million, but the Stones replied that this was a 'ludicrous figure' which, in their opinion, exceeded the collective earnings of the Beatles, Elvis Presley, the Rolling Stones and others.

Meanwhile 'Brown Sugar', first premiered at Altamont, was released as the new single, backed with 'Bitch'. In America both sides of the disc reached number 1, while in Britain it was only 'Brown Sugar' that made it to the top. Perhaps the added bonus of having 'Let It Rock' with 'Bitch' prevented the B-side from charting. Whatever the reason, the single was a hit, so it really wasn't that surprising that Decca rushed out a new compilation of old material. *Stone Age* was greeted with indifference by the Stones, who said they were not consulted and that the album was below the standard they were trying to keep up both in choice of content and cover design – but that didn't stop the massive sales.

Before leaving for France, Mick had stopped seeing Marianne. She was now living in Rome with Mario Schifano, an Italian film producer. However, there were rumours circulating that Mick was seeing a beautiful Nicaraguan model called Bianca.

In a conversation with BBC's *Scene And Heard* programme, Mick told Johnny Moran: 'What can I say but rumours, rumours, rumours?' And so it seemed until 12, May, when Mick married Bianca in St Tropez; first in a civil ceremony at the wedding chamber of the Town Hall, then in a Roman Catholic ceremony. 'At four in the afternoon,' reported Rolling Stone magazine, 'Mick and his bride-to-be, whose name on the wedding certificate is Bianca Rosa Perez-Mora, 26-year-old daughter of a Nicaraguan businessman, were still entrenched in the Byblos Hotel in the centre of St Tropez. They'd heard that 100 photographers were crammed into the wedding chamber of the local town hall, where the mayor was waiting to perform the civil ceremony. Mick wasn't going through with it unless "that lot" were cleared out. "Impossible," the mayor told anybody willing to listen. "The hall is a public place, and as such everyone had a legal right to be there". So fifty minutes late, protesting that he doesn't want to be married in a fish-bowl and surrounded by flying fists, agitated shrieks and popping flash bulbs, Mick arrived with his lady, Bianca Perez Moreno de Macias. After posing for photographers and facing the glare of television lights for several minutes, the couple went through a brief civil ceremony in the mayor's office. This was followed by a Roman Catholic ceremony performed by the Rev. Lucien Baud at the seventeenth century chapel of St Anne's. Jagger had been taking religious instruction from the Bishop of Frejus and from Father Lucien Baud, who conducted the service. A selection of tunes from *Love Story* was played on a harmonium, reportedly requested by Bianca. Roger Vadim and Natalie Delon were the witnesses. The reception, which did not end until 4 a.m., was held at the Café des Arts, where Steve Stills, Bobby Keys, Nicky Hopkins and Michael Shrieve and David Brown of Santana lead the jam session. Mick joined Doris Troy and P.P. Arnold in the chorus for a 25-minute soul-standard session. Mick would have liked the Stones to play but Keith was out of it, flat on his back, with his mouth open. Mrs Jagger told a reporter, 'I hope my other son doesn't become a superstar'. Les Perrin describes it as 'the most difficult day in my twenty-one years in the business'. After the reception, the yacht in the harbour whisked Mick and Bianca away on a cruising honeymoon in the small hours of the morning.

Following his return to St Tropez, Mick, with the rest of the Stones, began work on a new album. Nicky Hopkins, Bobby Keys, Jim Price and Gram Parson were brought in for the sessions that stretched out for a month, and even then, the finishing touches had to be taken care of in Hollywood. The Stones Mobile was only a recording facility; it had not been designed to accommodate sophisticated mixing techniques.

'It was the most difficult album I worked on with them,' recalls Jimmy Miller. 'I'm sure we would all agree. It was difficult for all of us for many reasons. The Stones were establishing a business set-up which they had to do with the proper tax structure, and so suddenly they found their heads into business which had to be taken care of. I can understand that, but I can also understand that it prevents a creative person from writing with the proficiency he would like when he's hung up every day with business affairs with lawyers and meetings, and with accountants meetings. So there was that problem, and there was the fact that Bianca was in the late stages of pregnancy during that period, so Mick was constantly in Paris, where Bianca was, while we were in the south of France, where we never really found a suitable place to record. We found various cinemas and public halls that one might rent, but we just never found a suitable site, and in the end we chose convenience, and went for the basement of Keith's house, which was at least a central point where everyone was living. But even then the Stones were quite spread out across the south of France. Between the two furthest points there were probably eight or nine hours of separation, so it was a little difficult to get everyone together for long periods of time, they'd get together for a few days and then everyone would naturally want to go home and see their families, so it wasn't the best conditions at all.

Mick's film 'Ned Kelly' premiered in Glenrowan, Australia (near where Kelly used to live), 1970 • Photo by Pictorial Press Ltd

'I remember we just couldn't seem to get started. Keith's basement was actually a lot of separate rooms that made up a basement and in the end, the separation was so poor that we'd have to have the piano in one room, and acoustic guitar in the basement kitchen because it had tiles, or had a nice ring. There was another room for the horns, and there was one main studio where the drums and Keith's amp were, and Bill would stand in there . . . but his amp would be out in the hall, and the wires would go out the door and down the hall, and all this was going into the mobile truck. Every time I wanted to communicate I would have to virtually run around to all the different rooms, and give the message. No, it wasn't a very nice experience, and I don't think that the work we did down there was among the most inspired work that the Stones have done.

'There was a lot of it, though, that's the thing. We ended up with quite a lot of work. "Ventilator Blues", oddly enough, is probably one of my favourites. I say "oddly enough" because I've never found many people who mention that track when they talk about the album, but the riff kind of got into my head. I remember it kept me up a few nights, and I used to think, well, that's a great simple riff.'

'Tumbling Dice' was the first single from the album to come out. It utilised the old blues ingredients of mixing lyrics about gambling and love. It preceded 'Exile On Main Street' by a couple of months.

Meanwhile, rehearsals for their next American tour got underway in Switzerland. The tour would start off in June and for the first time would employ 150 speakers and 16,000 watts of power.

Photo by Rex Features Ltd

The tour visited Vancouver, Seattle, San Francisco, Los Angeles, San Diego, Tucson, Albuquerque, Denver, Minnesota, Chicago, Kansas City, Fort Worth, Houston, Mobile and Tuscaloosa, and like all the other tours that had gone before, reports of wild incidents were the norm. At Vancouver 2,000 fans who were without tickets gatecrashed the Pacific Coliseum, resulting in thirty police officers being injured. The same hysteria was witnessed at San Diego with more riots causing injury to fifteen people and over sixty fans being arrested, and at Tucson, police used tear gas to disperse 300 fans trying to gatecrash the concert. 'It was a pretty wild tour,' teases Mick. 'Girls, drink, you name it, rock 'n' roll even; but your reason for being there is to do that two hours, or whatever it is, on the stage, so really your day is geared up to that. The rest of the time when you come off is geared to coming off that and travelling to the next one.'

For Charlie the thought of more touring was less appealing: 'I got off the plane after that tour and said no more because I don't actually like touring. I don't like living out of suitcases, and I hate being away from home. I always do tours thinking they're the last one, and at the end of them, I always leave the band. Because of what I do, I can't play the drums at home so I walk about, and to play the drums I have to go on the road, and to go on the road I have to leave home, and it's like a terrible vicious circle but it's always been my life.'

The second leg of the tour continued throughout July at Norfolk, Charlotte, Knoxville, St Louis, Akron, Indianapolis, Detroit, Toronto, Montreal, Boston, Philadelphia, Pittsburgh and New York, grossing over £1.5 million as the Stones played to more than three quarters of a million people.

'The tour was great; it was a lot of fun,' remembers Chris Odell. 'It was nice because you had everyone on one plane so there was not that confusion of dealing with commercial airlines. I remember very near the end of the tour, we were in Montreal, and going to Philadelphia, I believe, and Montreal was where there had been a bombing. They'd bombed one of the trucks. It was a little strange there, but we thought we'll go back to America and so we got on the plane, and the plane started to take off, when all of a sudden it stopped, and it pulled over to the left-hand side. The guy who was in charge of the guitars, Newman, immediately started yelling "There's a fire in the engine", and the pilot came back and said "No, there's not", but a lot of people were afraid of flying – Mick, I know is really terrified – so everyone was very uptight then. The pilot says "We're gonna try it again." So we go down the runway, ready to take off and the same thing happens again. So everyone's going "Let's get off this plane right now." The pilot says the meter which shows the speed that you need to take off and land wasn't working and that they can't take off without that, so Peter Rudge sent Allen Dunn and Jo Bergman off into the terminal to fix up commercial flights for the group to go on, and the rest of us had to stay in the plane. Peter put me in charge, made me social director, so I thought what do you do with a bunch of people like this who are really tired and in very bad moods, and also frightened out of their wits. So I got a megaphone and started telling jokes, and then someone found a football, an American football, and all the guys went out on the strip alongside the aeroplane, all the people that worked out in the terminals came running out and the football game started. Well, the American guys like Jim Price and Bobby Keys were playing very well, but the English guys didn't know how to play football, so it turned into a bit of a humorous event, and then the girls who were left in the plane were doing cheers, and so it brought the whole spirit up again after it was getting so low near the end of the tour. Everyone was really in great spirits, and by the time the plane was finally fixed about two or three hours later, everyone felt fantastic. The morale was really good.

Mick marries Bianca. Seen here with Mayor of St Tropez, Marius Astezan, 1971 • Photo by Popperfoto

'Farewell Concerts', 1971 • Photo by Popperfoto

Photo by Pictorial Press Ltd

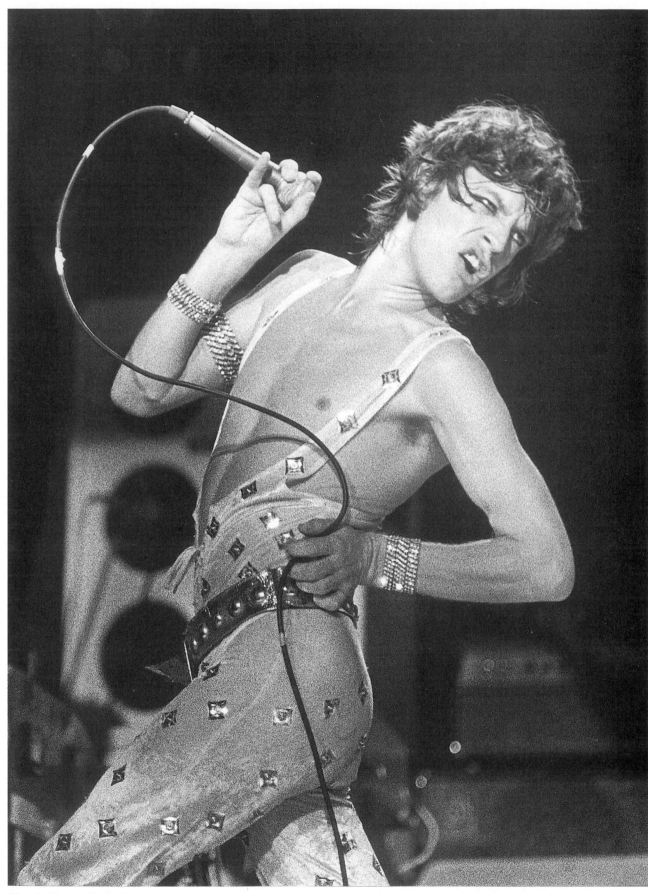

Photo by Fin Costello/Redferns

Photo by Pictorial Press Ltd

'Everyone did their best, including all of the Stones; they really liked the tour. I think it was one of the most enjoyable tours they'd done in a long time.'

Immediately after the tour, the Stones spent three weeks recording in Jamaica laying down tracks for their next album. 'One of the benefits of recording away from home in an isolated place like Jamaica is that there are no distractions,' recalls Mick. 'We can work without interruptions, although finding something to eat was a problem. We would usually get up too late for lunch and too early for dinner, and when we returned from the studio it was too early for breakfast.'

In the meantime, Decca put out an album of previously issued live material under the title of *Gimme Shelter* just as former co-manager Eric Easton announced in the High Court that he was suing Andrew Oldham, Allen Klein, Decca, London Records and Nanker Phelge Music.

The year 1973 looked to be less hectic as they kicked off with a concert at the Los Angeles Forum as a benefit for the victims of the Nicaraguan earthquake. This concert ranks as one of the most financially successful charity gigs in the history of popular music. 'LA station KMET-FM had a week-long telephone auction of Stones paraphernalia to further aid the Nicaraguans,' reported *Rolling Stone* magazine. 'Among the souvenirs was the studded velvet costume that Mick wore at the LA benefit. The starting price was $1,000 and it was autographed "To the owner, much love, Mick Jagger". Also on the block was the Rolling Stones tongue pillow that graced the stage during part of the last US tour, which Mick agreed to personally stain, somehow, to make it all the more valuable.'

From Los Angeles, the Stones flew out to Hawaii for two concerts in Honolulu before going on to Sydney for the start of their Australian tour. After this, Mick and Keith returned to Jamaica for a short while before flying out to the States. Bill went straight to California, Charlie to France, and Mick Taylor visited Indonesia.

On their return to London, the Stones went straight to Island studios to add the finishing touches to the *Goat's Head Soup* album, although for most of these sessions Keith was missing, which in retrospect was not surprising. He and Anita had been charged with possession of marijuana and firearms. Both were remanded on bail at Marylebone Magistrates Court on 31 July, although Keith was allowed to retain his passport for the duration of the Stones' European tour, which kicked off in September with rehearsals starting in Rotterdam in the middle of August. After the tour, Keith and Anita were fined and given conditional discharges.

In November, the Stones flew out to Munich to begin laying down tracks for their next album. The sessions at the Musicland Studio stretched through into December, and apart from a new single released in the States, not much else was happening.

Probably without realising it themselves, the Stones had just come through their first ten years.

Photo by London Features International Ltd

Photo by Redferns

Mick in 'Performance' • Photo by London Features International Ltd

'Ned Kelly' • Photo by Pictorial Press Ltd

Photo by Fin Costello/Redferns

Keith with Anita Pallenberg • Photo by Rex Features

Mick with Keith's wife, Anita Pallenberg, in the film 'Performance'
Photo by Pictorial Press Ltd

'Stargrove', Mick's house in Oxfordshire • Photo by Pictorial Press Ltd

Photo by Pictorial Press Ltd

Photo by Retna Pictures

Photo by Retna Pictures

Photo by Fin Costello/Redferns

Photo by Pictorial Press Ltd

Photo by Pictorial Press Ltd

Photo by Retna Pictures

Side 1:
ALL DOWN THE LINE
YOU CAN'T ALWAYS GET
WHAT YOU WANT
MIDNIGHT RAMBLER

Side 2:
BYE BYE JOHNNY
RIP THIS JOINT
LOVE IN VAIN
SWEET VIRGINIA
JUMPIN' JACK FLASH

RECORDED ON STAGE AT MADISON SQUARE GARDEN, JULY '72, NEW YORK
REAL STEREO TMQ 71060

USA Bootleg • Photo by Pictorial Press Ltd

Photo by Rex Features

Photo by Redferns

Photo by Pictorial Press Ltd

Photo by Retna Pictures

Chronology

1963

9 January
Charlie Watts joins the Rolling Stones.

28 April
Andrew Loog Oldham and Eric Easton see the Rolling Stones at Richmond and sign a management deal the next day.

3 May
The Stones sign with Decca Records.

10 May
First recording session at Olympic Studios. Andrew Oldham produces several tracks including 'Come On' and 'I Wanna Be Loved'.

7 June

The Stones' first single 'Come On'/'I Wanna Be Loved' released on Decca.

7 July

The Stones record their television debut for ATV's 'Thank Your Lucky Stars', which is broadcast six days later on 13 July.

29 September

First major British tour supporting the Everly Brothers and Bo Diddley, which opens at the New Victoria, London, with thirty dates concluding on 3 November.

1 November

'I Wanna Be Your Man'/'Stoned' released on Decca.

On HMS Discovery, 1963 • Photo by Pictorial Press Ltd

Photo by Pictorial Press Ltd

1 9 6 4

6 January

The Stones start their second tour, this time as the headlining act, supported by the Ronettes, Marty Wilde, Dave Berry and the Swinging Blue Jeans among others.

17 January

'The Rolling Stones' EP released on Decca.

8 February — 7 March

The Stones begin their third British tour, with support acts including John Leyton, Mike Berry, Jet Harris, the Innocents and Billie Davis among others.

21 February
New single 'Not Fade Away'/'Little By Little' is released.

16 April
Decca releases the first album, 'The Rolling Stones'.

3 – 20 June
First American tour.

Charlie and Bill with Andrew Oldham on the set of 'Ready Steady Go' • Photo by Pictorial Press Ltd

16 June

The Stones fly to Magdalene College, Oxford to honour an agreement booked the previous year and then immediately resume their US tour.

26 June

Release of 'It's All Over Now'/'Good Times, Bad Times'.

8 July

'It's All Over Now' goes to number 1.

5 September

British tour with Charlie and Inez Foxx until 11 October.

20 October

The Olympia is the band's first show in Paris and hundreds of stampeding fans break windows at the theatre after the show. Police are called in; there are riots in the streets, resulting in 150 people arrested.

23 October

The Stones fly to the USA for twelve dates, including the Academy of Music and the 'The Ed Sullivan Show'.

13 November

Release of 'Little Red Rooster'/'Off The Hook'.

21 December

Publication of pocket book 'Ode To A High Flying Bird' by Charlie Watts. It is the story of legendary sax player Charlie 'Bird' Parker and was written in 1961.

1 9 6 5

15 January

Release of 'The Rolling Stones No. 2' album.

26 February

Release of 'The Last Time'/'Play With Fire'.

5 March – 18 April

Major European tour with the Hollies, included stops in England, Scandinavia and France.

Photo by Pictorial Press Ltd

22 April

Fly to Montreal for Canadian and American tour.

20 August

Release of 'Satisfaction'/'Spider And The Fly'.

24 August

The Rolling Stones meet Allen Klein for the first time.

28 August

Andrew Oldham and Allen Klein to co-manage the Rolling Stones. The band sign a new five-year contract with Decca.

17 October

Release of the album 'Out Of Our Heads'.

22 October

Release of 'Get Off My Cloud'/'The Singer Not The Song'.

29 October

Again, fly to Montreal for the fourth Canadian/American tour.

Photo by Pictorial Press Ltd

1 9 6 6

4 February

Release of 'Nineteenth Nervous Breakdown'/'As Tears Go By'.

26 March

European tour begins.

15 April

Release of 'Aftermath' album.

13 May

Release of 'Paint It Black'/'Long While'.

Royal Albert Hall, 1966. The group had to vacate due to fans invading the stage • Photo by Pictorial Press Ltd

Photo by Pictorial Press Ltd

23 June

Rolling Stones arrive in New York for their fifth American/Canadian tour, which ends in Hawaii.

10 September

The Rolling Stones appear on 'The Ed Sullivan Show' in New York, and 'Ready Steady Go' in England.

23 September

Release of 'Have You Seen Your Mother Baby?'/'Who's Driving Your Plane?'

23 September – 9 October

Opening of British tour at London's Albert Hall with reception afterwards. Tour with Ike and Tina Turner and the Yardbirds.

4 November

Release of 'Big Hits (High Tide And Green Grass)' compilation album.

1967

20 January

Release of 'Between The Buttons' album in America.

28 January

Release of 'Let's Spend The Night Together'/'Ruby Tuesday'.

25 March – 13 April

Opening of European tour in Oerbo, Sweden. The Stones make their first visit behind the Iron Curtain when they play Warsaw, Poland.

18 August

Release of 'We Love You'/'Dandelion' – described as a thank-you to fans who were loyal during their various court appearances.

29 September

The Rolling Stones announce that they have broken away from Andrew Oldham and will in future produce their own records.

21 December

Release of 'Their Satanic Majesties' Request' album.

Charlie Watts with daughter, Serafina • Photo by Pictorial Press Ltd

1968

25 May

Release of 'Jumping Jack Flash'/'Child Of The Moon'.

1 September

Mick begins work on his first film role in Nic Roeg's 'Performance'.

5 December

The Rolling Stones hold a beggars' banquet at Elizabethan rooms in London to mark the release of their album 'Beggars' Banquet'. Lord Harlech deputises for Keith, who is ill. They surprise guests with a custard pie throwing party.

12 December

The Rolling Stones Rock 'n' Roll Circus is filmed at Wembley studios for television. Friends include John and Yoko Lennon. 'Beggars' Banquet' is released.

Brian with Motown singing star Diana Ross, 1968 • Photo by Pictorial Press Ltd

Rock 'n' Roll Circus • Photos by Rex Features

1 9 6 9

8 June

Brian Jones leaves the Rolling Stones. Former Yardbirds guitarist Mick Taylor replaces him.

3 July

Brian Jones dies at his home near Hartfield (Cotchford Farm).

5 July

Rolling Stones perform a free concert in London's Hyde Park. Mick Jagger reads a poem by Shelley as a dedication to Brian and releases thousands of butterflies.

6 July

Mick Jagger leaves for Australia to film 'Ned Kelly'.

11 July

Release of 'Honky Tonk Women'/'You Can't Always Get What You Want'.

12 September

Release of 'Through The Past Darkly' album.

17 October

The Rolling Stones arrive in Los Angeles to set up their sixth American tour.

7 November

Stones begin their US tour.

5 December

Release of 'Let It Bleed' album.

Photo by Redferns

Photo by Pictorial Press Ltd

1970

28 July

Premiere of 'Ned Kelly' in Glenrowan, Melbourne, Australia (near where the real Ned Kelly used to live).

30 July

The Rolling Stones inform Allen Klein that neither he nor ABKCO Industries Inc., nor any other company have any authority to negotiate contracts on their behalf in the future.

19 September

Release of 'Performance' soundtrack album, featuring Mick Jagger, with Ry Cooder, Randy Newman and Buffy Saint Marie. Release of 'Get Yer Ya Yas Out' live album.

7 November

Release of 'Memo To Turner'/'Natural Magic' – a solo by Mick Jagger from the 'Performance' soundtrack.

1 9 7 1

23 April

Release of 'Sticky Fingers' album, the first on Rolling Stones Records. Cover design is by Andy Warhol. Decca releases 'Stone Age' album.

31 July

Premiere of film 'Gimme Shelter' at the Rialto Cinema in London.

20 August

Release on Rolling Stones label of Howlin' Wolf session in London, which includes Bill and Charlie.

27 August

Decca Records releases 'Gimme Shelter' album, which is a collection of oldies mainly taken from live concerts.

Photo by Pictorial Press Ltd

1972

12 April

Release of 'Exile On Main Street' album.

14 April

Release of 'Tumblin' Dice'/'Sweet Black Angel'.

29 May

'Brown Sugar' hits number 1 in the US charts.

30 June – 26 July

Seventh American/Canadian tour opens in Vancouver, British Colombia, and includes stops in San Diego, Tucson, Albuquerque, Washington, DC, Montreal and New York.

30 June

Decca Records releases a maxi-single – 'Street Fighting Man'/'Surprise'/ 'Everybody Needs Somebody To Love'.

1 9 7 3

18 January

LA Forum – the Rolling Stones hold a concert in aid of the earthquake victims of Nicaragua.

29 April

Decca releases old recording of 'Sad Day'.

20 August

Release of 'Angie'/'Silver Train'.

31 August

Release of 'Goat's Head Soup' album.

1 September – 19 October

European tour begins at the Stadthalle, Vienna. Yuri Kurinoff, a representative of the Soviet Union's Ministry of Culture, attends the show. Other stops include Cologne, London, Manchester, Glasgow, Berne, Munich, Frankfurt, Hamburg, Gothenburg, Copenhagen, Rotterdam, Brussels and Berlin.

Photo by Retna Pictures

UK Album Discography 1963–1973

DECCA LK 4577
READY, STEADY, GO! Compilation
Stones tracks: Come On/I Wanna Be Your Man
(January 1964)

DECCA LK 4577
SATURDAY CLUB Compilation
Stones tracks: Poison Ivy/Fortune Teller
(January 1964)

DECCA LK 4605
THE ROLLING STONES
Route 66/I Just Want To Make Love To You/Honest I Do/I Need You Baby
Now I've Got A Witness/Little By Little/I'm A King Bee/Tell Me
Can I Get A Witness?/You Can Make It If You Try/Walking The Dog
(April 1964)

DECCA LK 4661
THE ROLLING STONES No. 2
Everybody Needs Somebody To Love/Down Home Girl/You Can't Catch Me
Time Is On My Side/What A Shame/Grown Up Wrong
Down The Road A Piece/Under The Boardwalk/I Can't Be Satisfied
Pain In My Heart/Off The Hook/Susie-Q
(January 1965)

DECCA LK 4733
OUT OF OUR HEADS

She Said Yeah/Mercy Mercy/Hitch Hike/That's How Strong My Love Is
Good Times/Gotta Get Away/Talkin' Bout You/Cry To Me/Oh Baby
Heart Of Stone/The Under Assistant West Coast Promotion Man/I'm Free
(September 1965)

DECCA SKL 4786
AFTERMATH

Mother's Little Helper/Stupid Girl/Lady Jane/Under My Thumb
Doncha Bother Me/Goin' Home/Flight 505/High And Dry/Out Of Time
It's Not Easy/I Am Waiting/Take It Or Leave It/Think/What To Do
(April 1966)

DECCA TXS 101
BIG HITS (HIGH TIDE AND GREEN GRASS)
Compilation

Have You Seen Your Mother Baby, Standing In The Shadow?/Paint It Black
It's All Over Now/The Last Time/Heart Of Stone/Not Fade Away/Come On
Satisfaction/Get Off My Cloud/As Tears Go By/Nineteenth Nervous
Breakdown/Lady Jane/Time Is On My Side/Little Red Rooster
(November 1966)

DECCA LK 4852
BETWEEN THE BUTTONS

Yesterday's Papers/My Obsession/Back Street Girl/Connection
She Smiles Sweetly/Cool, Calm And Collected/All Sold Out
Please Go Home/Who's Been Sleeping Here?/Complicated
Miss Amanda Jones/Something Happened To Me Yesterday
(January 1967)

DECCA TXS 103
THEIR SATANIC MAJESTIES' REQUEST

Sing This All Together/Citadel/In Another Land/2,000 Man
She's A Rainbow/The Lantern/Gomper/2,000 Light Years From Home
On With The Show
(December 1967)

DECCA SKL 4955
BEGGARS' BANQUET
Sympathy For The Devil/No Expectations/Dear Doctor/Parachute Woman
Street Fighting Man/Prodigal Son/Stray Cat Blues/Factory Girl
Salt Of The Earth
(December 1968)

DECCA SKL 5019
THROUGH THE PAST DARKLY (Big Hits Vol. 2)
Compilation
Jumping Jack Flash/Mother's Little Helper/2,000 Light Years From Home
Let's Spend The Night Together/You Better Move On/We Love You
Street Fighting Man/She's A Rainbow/Ruby Tuesday/Dandelion
Sittin' On The Fence/Honky Tonk Women
(September 1969)

DECCA SKL 5025
LET IT BLEED
Gimme Shelter/Love In Vain/Country Honk/Live With Me/Let It Bleed
Midnight Rambler/You Got The Silver/Monkey Man
You Can't Always Get What You Want
(December 1969)

DECCA SKL 5065
GET YER YA-YAS OUT! Live
Jumping Jack Flash/Carol/Stray Cat Blues/Love In Vain
Midnight Rambler/Sympathy For The Devil/Live With Me/Little Queenie
Honky Tonk Woman/Street Fighting Man
(September 1970)

ROLLING STONES COC 59100
STICKY FINGERS
Brown Sugar/Sway/Wild Horses/Can't You Hear Me Knocking?
You Gotta Move/Bitch/I Got The Blues/Sister Morphine/Dead Flowers
Moonlight Mile
(April 1971)

Photo by Pictorial Press Ltd

DECCA SKL 5084
STONE AGE Compilation
*Look What You've Done/It's All Over Now/Confessin' The Blues
One More Try/As Tears Go By/The Spider And The Fly/My Girl
Paint It Black/If You Need Me/The Last Time/Blue Turns To Grey
Around And Around
(April 1971)*

ROLLING STONES COC 69100
EXILE ON MAIN STREET Double Album
*Rocks Off/Rip This Joint/Shake Your Hips/Casino Boogie/Tumbling Dice
Sweet Virginia/Torn And Frayed/Sweet Black Angel/Loving Cup/Happy
Turd On The Run/Ventilator Blues/I Just Want To See His Face
Let It Loose/All Down The Line/Stop Breaking Down/Shine A Light
Soul Survivor
(May 1972)*

DECCA SKL 5101
GIMME SHELTER Compilation
*Jumping Jack Flash/Love In Vain/Honky Tonk Women/Street Fighting Man
Sympathy For The Devil/Gimme Shelter/Under My Thumb
Time Is On My Side/I've Been Loving You Too Long/Fortune Teller
Lady Jane/Satisfaction
(October 1972)*

ROLLING STONES COC 59101
GOAT'S HEAD SOUP
*Dancing With Mr D/100 Years Ago/Coming Down Again
Doo Doo Doo Doo/Angie/Silver Train/Hide Your Love/Winter
Can You Hear The Music?/Star Star
(August 1973)*

Photo by Retna Pictures